MONOGRAPHS OF THE
SOCIETY FOR RESEARCH IN
CHILD DEVELOPMENT

*Serial No. 253, Vol. 63, No. 1, 1998*

W9-AEH-635

# BEYOND LABELING:
# THE ROLE OF MATERNAL INPUT
# IN THE ACQUISITION OF
# RICHLY STRUCTURED CATEGORIES

*Susan A. Gelman*
*John D. Coley*
*Karl S. Rosengren*
*Erin Hartman*
*Athina Pappas*

WITH COMMENTARY BY
*Frank C. Keil*

MONOGRAPHS OF THE SOCIETY FOR RESEARCH IN CHILD DEVELOPMENT
*Serial No. 253, Vol. 63, No. 1, 1998*

# CONTENTS

# ABSTRACT

GELMAN, SUSAN A.; COLEY, JOHN D.; ROSENGREN, KARL S.; HARTMAN, ERIN; and
PAPPAS, ATHINA. Beyond Labeling: The Role of Maternal Input in the
Acquisition of Richly Structured Categories. *Monographs of the Society for
Research in Child Development*, 1998, **63**(1, Serial No. 253).

Recent research shows that preschool children are skilled classifiers, using categories both to organize information efficiently and to extend knowledge beyond what is already known. Moreover, by 2½ years of age, children
are sensitive to nonobvious properties of categories and assume that category
members share underlying similarities. Why do children expect categories to
have this rich structure, and how do children appropriately limit this expectation to certain domains (i.e., animals vs. artifacts)?

The present studies explore the role of maternal input, providing one
of the first detailed looks at how mothers convey information about category
structure during naturalistic interactions. Forty-six mothers and their 20- or
35-month-old children read picture books together. Sessions were videotaped, and the resulting transcripts were coded for explicit and implicit discussion of animal and artifact categories. Sequences of gestures toward pictures were also examined in order to reveal the focus of attention and implicit
links drawn between items.

Results indicate that mothers provided a rich array of information beyond simple labeling routines. Taxonomic categories were stressed in subtle
and indirect ways, in both speech and gesture, especially for animals. Statements and gestures that linked two pictures were more frequent for taxonomically related animal pictures than for other picture pairs. Mothers also generalized category information using generic noun phrases, again more for
animals than for artifacts. However, mothers provided little explicit discussion
of nonobvious similarities, underlying properties, or inductive potential
among category members. These data suggest possible mechanisms by which
a notion of *kind* is conveyed in the absence of detailed information about
category essences.

# I. INTRODUCTION

Preschool children are skilled classifiers, using categories both to organize information efficiently and to extend knowledge beyond what is already known. Moreover, by 2½ years of age, children are sensitive to nonobvious properties of categories and often expect category members to share underlying similarities. Why and how do children's categories come to have the structure that they do? In this *Monograph,* we focus on what kinds of information parents provide. Although children receive information relevant to categories and conceptual structure from many sources other than parents, parental input is presumed to be particularly salient and important during the preschool years. Studying parental input is a first step toward learning about the child's contribution (Callanan, 1991; Keil, 1989). By examining what parents say—and what they fail to say—we can better understand the possible roles of both parent and child in constructing categories.

## CHILDREN'S EARLY UNDERSTANDING OF CATEGORIES

Categories are critical for organizing and extending knowledge (Smith & Medin, 1981). They allow us to identify things in the world, store ideas efficiently in memory, create analogies and solve problems, and draw inferences beyond what is already known (Gelman & Medin, 1993). At least two of the basic functions of categories are present even before children begin to speak: that of grouping information efficiently (Mehler & Fox, 1985) and that of fostering inferences about the unknown (Baldwin, Markman, & Melartin, 1993; Hayne, Rovee-Collier, & Perris, 1987). Given how early these capacities emerge and their centrality in any form of intelligent thought, these basic processes are likely to be innate and not to require any special teaching or encouragement on the part of caregivers.

However, at some point during the preschool years, children come to appreciate two additional and crucial aspects of categories: (*a*) that categories can be richly structured,[1] capturing abundant clusters of information and promoting important inferences about unknown and/or nonobvious properties, and (*b*) that only some categories are organized in this manner (Callanan, 1990; Gelman, 1988; Markman, 1989). We review the evidence for both these understandings below.

## Richly Structured Categories

Human categories are distinctive in their responsiveness to knowledge and experience. One of the more striking manifestations of this sort of openness is that certain categories incorporate nonobvious information that is tied to naive theories, or folk explanations of how the world works (Barrett, Abdi, Murphy, & Gallagher, 1993; Gelman, 1996; Murphy & Medin, 1985). Quine (1969) notes that, although we can classify instances on the basis of such theory-neutral resemblances as color or shape, we also have the capacity to alter such groupings to incorporate the insights of knowledge and experience. Although intuitive resemblances are available to all species, theory-laden categories may be unique to humans. Quine gives the example *marsupial rats*, which look like rats but, on subtle biological examination, are classified within the kangaroo family.

Children certainly do not possess scientific theories (Brewer & Samarapungavan, 1991; Kuhn, 1989), yet they seem to form "commonsense" theories in several domains (see Carey, 1995; Gopnik & Wellman, 1994; Wellman & Gelman, 1992). Moreover, support for Quine's insight comes from a variety of observations of concepts, from philosophers, linguists, and psychol-

---

[1] A closely related, although distinct, claim is that certain categories are "richly structured" in the sense of representing correlated attributes. This is particularly true of *basic-level* natural language categories, such as *chair, elephant,* or *computer* (Mervis & Rosch, 1981; Rosch, Mervis, Gray, Johnson, & Boyes-Braem, 1976). Basic-level categories fall at an intermediate level of abstraction between more abstract, superordinate categories (e.g., *furniture*) and more specific, subordinate-level categories (e.g., *rocking chair*). They capture especially many distinctive features, relative to other levels of abstraction. Members of any given basic-level category have correlated properties, are similar to one another in shape, and are interacted with in predictable ways (e.g., chairs are sat on). The basic level is the default level of naming and is processed more efficiently than other levels of categorization. Basic-level categories are of particular interest from a developmental perspective because they are the categories learned earliest in language (Horton & Markman, 1980; Markman & Callanan, 1984; Waxman & Gelman, 1986; although see Mandler & Bauer, 1988). The relation between richly structured categories in the sense discussed here and basic-level categories is indirect and not fully explored. Although many—perhaps most—richly structured categories are basic level (e.g., animal kinds), there are also many basic-level categories that are arguably not theory laden (e.g., *basket, nail*). Thus, in order to address the question of how children acquire richly structured categories, it is relevant but not sufficient to examine the input children hear regarding basic-level categories.

ogists (Gelman & Coley, 1991; see also Jevons, 1877; Keil, 1986, 1987, 1989, 1994; Kripke, 1971, 1972; Markman, 1991; Mill, 1846; Murphy & Medin, 1985; Putnam, 1970; Rips, 1989; Shipley, 1993). Specifically, these investigations reveal three aspects of richly structured categories: they have rich inductive potential, capture nonobvious properties, and are treated as if they have essences. Importantly, these properties hold true for categories acquired by young children as well as those of adults.

### Rich Inductive Potential

Members of a category may share indefinitely many properties. For example, cats are alike, not just in ways that can be immediately perceived (e.g., shape, fur, whiskers), but also in nonobvious ways (e.g., anatomical structure, means of reproduction, brain chemistry) about which ordinary adults continue to learn and to which experts (such as biologists) devote lifetimes of study. Because of these shared similarities, facts learned about a single instance often generalize to the kind.

Studies with children demonstrate that 2–5-year-olds readily draw inductive inferences from one category member to another (Gelman & O'Reilly, 1988), even in the strong case when outward appearances are conflicting (Gelman & Coley, 1990; Gelman & Markman, 1986, 1987). For example, on learning that a stegosaurus (*dinosaur*) has cold blood and a bird has warm blood, preschool children will infer that a pterodactyl (also labeled a *dinosaur*) has cold blood, even though it more closely resembles the bird. Before school age, children expect category members to share important underlying commonalities that are not immediately apparent.

### Nonobvious Properties

Categories may promote inductions because they share properties that cannot always be readily observed. Moreover, underlying similarities or differences are not always reflected in surface appearances, leading to appearance-reality conflicts.[2] One member of a richly structured category may not necessarily resemble other category members (e.g., an ostrich does not look like a robin or a bluejay) and may even appear to be something else altogether

---

[2] Appearance-reality conflicts are also found in categories that are not richly structured. For example, a valuables container can be made to resemble a book. However, with artifacts, the conflict is typically deliberate, and one can readily resolve the conflict by consulting the creator's intent (see Bloom, 1996). In contrast, with richly structured categories, an appearance-reality conflict is inferred despite the lack of any deliberate deception and, to the average speaker, is more difficult to uncover. There is no simple rule that can resolve such cases.

(e.g., an insect camouflaged to look like a leaf). The ultimate arbiters of category membership are the nonobvious properties shared by ostriches, robins, and bluejays or by leaf insects and other insects rather than by leaf insects and leaves.

Preschool children's sensitivity to nonobvious properties can be seen in various ways: in their attention to internal parts (Gelman, 1990; Gelman, Durgin, & Kaufman, 1995; Gelman & Gottfried, 1996; Gelman & O'Reilly, 1988; Johnson & Wellman, 1982; Simons & Keil, 1995); in their reasoning about nonvisible or invisible entities, including germs, mental states, and dissolved particles (Au, Sidle, & Rollins, 1993; Kalish, 1996b; Rosen & Rozin, 1993; Siegal, 1988; Wellman, 1990); in their comprehension of appearance-reality contrasts (Flavell, Flavell, & Green, 1983); and in their judgments about identity (Gelman & Wellman, 1991; Gutheil & Rosengren, 1996; Keil, 1989). Children realize that, for animals, internal parts (which are inherently nonobvious) differ from external parts (Gelman, 1990) and can be critical in determining an object's identity and how it functions (Gelman & Wellman, 1991; Keil, 1989). Children also appreciate that animals have innate potential for certain behavioral and physical properties (e.g., shape of tail, movement pattern; Gelman & Wellman, 1991) and that certain properties (e.g., kinds of internal organs) are inherited (Hirschfeld, 1995b; Springer & Keil, 1989).

### Psychological Essentialism

Certain categories are treated as if they have an underlying reality or true nature (an "essence") that one cannot observe directly but that gives an object its identity and is responsible for other similarities that category members share (James, 1890; Locke, 1894/1959; Medin, 1989). For gold, it is the atomic mass of 196.97; for tigers, it is perhaps a particular genetic structure (but see Malt, 1994). Note that this is a psychological claim, not a metaphysical or a linguistic claim. Although many philosophers and biologists question whether categories truly have essences (e.g., Mayr, 1988), ordinary speakers treat them as if they do (Atran, 1990; Gelman, Coley, & Gottfried, 1994; Medin & Ortony, 1989). Moreover, in many (perhaps nearly all) cases, the hypothesized "essence" is not known by the ordinary language user. Instead, people have an essence placeholder (Medin, 1989). In other words, they hold the intuitive belief that an essence exists, even if its details have not yet been revealed. Thus, an essence typically could not be part of the semantic core of a word, nor could it determine word extensions. Nonetheless, it has implications for people's beliefs regarding the depth and stability of a concept (Rothbart & Taylor, 1990). Essentialist reasoning is implicit in preschool children's judgments that an animal's identity is retained over even dramatic transformations (e.g., caterpillar to butterfly; Keil, 1989; Rosengren,

Gelman, Kalish, & McCormick, 1991). It is also implicit in preschoolers' judgments that animals have innate potential to exhibit various physical and behavioral characteristics (e.g., that a helpless tiger cub will grow to be fierce, even if raised by sheep; Gelman & Wellman, 1991).

Categories with inductive potential, nonobvious properties, and a presumption of essence are richly structured in the sense that they presuppose a reality beyond the phenomenal. In other words, theoretical constructs provide a "truer" representation of reality than what can be observed, and the world is organized into densely complex and predictive clusters of correlated features. These complex clusters are precisely the categories that are identified and named in language. To give an example, when we classify an animal as a turtle, we are interested in much more than its outward appearance. We typically assume that this classification may have a nonobvious basis (e.g., although the presence of a shell or particular markings may be useful when classifying a turtle, these features can be overridden by other, more "biological" properties), an essence (e.g., turtle DNA), rich inductive potential (e.g., regarding body temperature, number of offspring typically produced, means of gathering food), and openness to revision. We presume that there may be turtles that look like rocks (but are not), and rocks that look like turtles (but are not), or that one could discover new species of turtles that are unusually tiny or unusually large or that don't even have distinct shells.

The research cited above does not imply that perceptual similarity is not important to children's concepts. Appearances are clearly salient and important in many contexts and on many tasks (Jones & Smith, 1993). Even within an essentialist framework, appearances provide crucial cues regarding an underlying essence (Gelman & Medin, 1993). Nevertheless, evidence strongly suggests that preschool children assume that some categories are structured in ways that cannot be characterized in terms of perceptual information alone.

### Differences among Categories

Children's assumptions about nonobvious properties, category essences, and inductive potential have been demonstrated most fully for animal categories (see above). In addition, adults and children appear to have similar expectations about such social categories as gender and race (Hirschfeld, 1995a, 1995b; Taylor, 1996), about disease concepts (Kalish, 1996a), about nonbiological natural kinds (Gelman & Markman, 1986), and even (for adults at least) about personality traits (Yuill, 1992). However, not all categories have the properties described above (Markman, 1989; Mill, 1846). Where direct comparisons of animals and human-made artifacts have been conducted, clear domain differences have been found as early as 3 or 4 years of age.

These comparisons include studies of internal parts (Gelman, 1990; Gelman & O'Reilly, 1988; Simons & Keil, 1995), object identity (Keil, 1989), inheritance (Hirschfeld, 1995b; Springer, 1992; Springer & Keil, 1989), origins (Gelman & Kremer, 1991; Keil, 1989), self-generated movement (Gelman et al., 1995; Massey & Gelman, 1988), and spontaneous growth and healing (Backscheider, Shatz, & Gelman, 1993; Rosengren et al., 1991).

Specifically, animals are assumed to have richly structured internal parts that differ from their exteriors and are responsible for self-generated movement. In contrast, it is assumed that simple artifacts have the same parts inside as outside and that the inner parts are unrelated to movement. Similarly, it is assumed that superficial changes cannot alter the identity of an animal but can alter the identity of an artifact. Again, animals are thought to inherit such properties as skin color and physique through the biological parents, whereas no such process is possible for artifacts. Origins for animals implicate a natural, self-generated, inherent process; origins for artifacts implicate a human or human-like "other" who creates the item (Bloom, 1996). Finally, growth and healing in animals are assumed to be highly patterned, predictable processes stemming from the animal itself. The terms *growth* and *healing* do not, however, even typically apply to artifacts; moreover, changes over time and mending are accomplished in a less predictable way for artifacts and require external agents of change.

Thus, much recent evidence suggests that children's early categories are richly structured but that this rich structure is selectively applied in some domains and not others. We now review what is known about parental input, in order to uncover the developmental origins of this early category structure.

## Potential Role of Parental Input

Although much is known about the structure of children's early categories, relatively little is known about the origins of that structure. Formal schooling can be ruled out as a necessary precursor for richly structured categories since by age 2½ children appreciate the inductive potential of categories despite not yet having attended school (Gelman & Coley, 1990). What, then, are the developmental precedents for the appreciation that categories can be richly structured but that only some categories have this form?

We focus on two possible uses of parental input data, discussed by Callanan (1991). First, patterns of input can provide potential data to the child. In other words, by characterizing the input, we discover what sorts of knowledge children are exposed to and so in principle what children could be acquiring from others. Second, patterns of input can reveal parent-child mismatches. If children's concepts exhibit properties not evident in the input, this suggests places where children may have a priori biases (accurate or inaccurate) that operate in the absence of relevant input.

In examining these issues, it is important to avoid dichotomizing explanations of category acquisition and development into the opposition of "learned" and "innate." Explanations do not lie along a unidimensional continuum (Marler, 1991). Indeed, parental input and children's biases may work together toward a common goal (Markman, 1992), with children's interpretive biases and parents' structuring of the input acting in consistent and mutually reinforcing ways.

In sum, an examination of the role of parental input potentially informs theories of conceptual development. Clearly, parental naming patterns influence categorical structure by demarcating category boundaries. However, labels alone may not explain the rich structure evident in preschoolers' categories. A further examination of the informational content of parental speech and mismatches between parental speech and children's concepts is crucial to explaining how children's concepts come selectively to exhibit rich structure. A detailed look at the *nature* of input also is necessary for future work to examine the *effects* of input.

## REVIEW OF RESEARCH ON PARENTAL INPUT ABOUT CATEGORIES

### Labeling

Much of the research on parental input to children's concepts focuses on parental patterns of labeling. (Although the extensive literatures on syntactic and phonological input are pertinent to questions regarding language development, they are not directly relevant here.) Parents frequently label objects and pictures for their children, particularly at the basic level, although context influences the level of naming, with variations due either to activity type (e.g., book reading vs. mealtime) or to array of referents available (Adams & Bullock, 1986; Blewitt, 1983; Lucariello & Nelson, 1986; Mervis & Mervis, 1982; Wales, Colman, & Pattison, 1983; White, 1982).

Labeling appears to be an important way of conveying category membership to young children (Gelman & Markman, 1986). Through language, children can learn to redraw category boundaries. For example, naming a pterodactyl a *dinosaur* changes the type of inferences that young children make about the animal (Gelman & Coley, 1990). Parents also convey important information by avoiding certain constructions, deliberately making "errors," and spending much more time on certain kinds of labels than on others. For example, parents rarely use superordinate-level labels for atypical items (White, 1982). They label homonyms in unambiguous ways (Kohn & Landau, 1990). They make overextensions that are consistent with children's level of knowledge, such as calling various round things *balls* (Mervis, 1987). They guide the child, naming whole objects and not parts of objects (Ninio, 1980), and providing different sentence frames when introducing superordinate- as opposed to basic- or subordinate-level names (Callanan, 1985, 1989).

Moreover, children make use of the information that parents provide, in order to acquire new words (Mervis & Mervis, 1988; Snow & Goldfield, 1983). For example, parents demonstrate different naming patterns when introducing basic-level as opposed to superordinate-level words (e.g., *mixer* vs. *machine*), and children interpret these different patterns appropriately (Callanan, 1989). Similarly, parents' tendency to point to and label whole objects instead of parts (Ninio & Bruner, 1978) is matched by children's expectation that labels will refer to whole objects instead of parts (Markman, 1989). Thus, parental labeling practices help children learn the structure of lexical hierarchies, disambiguate potentially confusing labels, and scaffold the acquisition of potentially difficult items.

If children make the dual assumptions that (1) common nouns mark categories and that (2) categories are richly structured, then mere labeling could result in richly structured categories (Carey, 1995, pp. 276–277; Macnamara, 1986). In favor of this position, one could argue that children's tendency to treat category labels as mutually exclusive (i.e., assuming that each object has only one label) reflects their overapplication of this linkage between count nouns and categories with underlying essences (Carey, 1995).

However, as discussed earlier, children are selective about which categories are richly structured, and labeling by itself does not differentiate between richly structured categories and others. Not all labels map directly onto theory-rich, or even coherent, categories. For example, *dog* is a richly structured category, but *furniture* is not, nor is *pet*. Likewise, homonyms (*bat*) and metaphoric uses (*bear*) include instances that share few similarities with other instances. Although richly structured categories may be more likely to be lexicalized (e.g., *cat* vs. *things that begin with the letter "c"*), neither adults nor children simply assume that objects given the same word fall into a richly structured category. For example, Davidson and Gelman (1990) found that 4-year-old children did not treat a new label as naming a kind when within-category similarity was too low. Thus, children make use of multiple sources of information (at the very least naming patterns and perceptual information) to determine which categories are richly structured.

### Gestures

Another means of providing information is with gestures. (Here we focus on nonlinguistic gestures in hearing children and parents, rather than on the gestural systems of sign languages, such as American Sign Language.) Nonlinguistic gestures are not simply mirrors of spoken language (Alibali &

Goldin-Meadow, 1993; McNeill, 1992; Perry, Church, & Goldin-Meadow, 1988; Shatz, 1982). Gesture sequences do not map directly onto the syntax of spoken language (Schaffer, Hepburn, & Collis, 1983; Shatz, 1982), nor do they help young children interpret speech more accurately (Schnur & Shatz, 1984). Gestures can contain specific information that is not present in speech—and may not even be consciously available (Alibali & Goldin-Meadow, 1993; Perry et al., 1988). Thus, gestures can repeat, contradict, augment, illustrate, or accent information presented verbally (Ekman & Friesen, 1969).

One type of gesture commonly used by both parents and children is pointing. From an early age children are receptive to information supplemental to labeling that is provided in parental pointing gestures. Infants as young as 9 months appropriately interpret adults' points by looking in the indicated direction (Bates, Benigni, Bretherton, Camaioni, & Volterra, 1979). Ninio (1980) found that there is an implicit structure in parental ostensive gestures: when parents point to pictures and name them, they most typically refer to the entire depicted object rather than a part. She notes that, although ostensive points are logically ambiguous, they "are made unambiguous by this 'rule of the complete object'" (p. 572). Children appear to be sensitive to this convention, inferring that labels provided by "ostensive definition" (pointing and labeling) are words for whole objects (Markman, 1989). Baldwin and Markman (1989) find that 10–14-month-old children look much longer toward an object that has been pointed to than toward a distractor object, although the combined activity of naming plus pointing enhances children's attention and word learning even further.

In addition to interpreting points in a consistent manner, children begin pointing early in life (Fenson et al., 1994), and their pointing undergoes important developments in the first 2 years. Murphy (1978) found that 9-month-old infants are able to point at pictures in picture books with their mothers. By 14 months of age, infants integrate pointing with vocal activity. By 20 months of age, amount of pointing increases dramatically, and children are beginning to combine points into "strings," in which one point leads directly into the next with no break in between.

Children also use gestures beyond simple pointing (McNeill, 1992). For example, some hearing children invent simple gestural "signs" to refer to particular concepts (Acredolo & Goodwyn, 1988; Bates et al., 1979). Children also vary their use of gestures to fit the context (e.g., appropriately using more gestures with pronouns than with nouns; Tomasello, Anselmi, & Farrar, 1984/1985). At this point, however, little is known about parental gestures beyond pointing.

In sum, parents appear to use pointing gestures to augment and clarify ostensive labeling. Parents may well use other kinds of gestures to highlight

9

relations between objects or to call attention to salient perceptual features of objects. One goal of the present *Monograph* is to examine these issues further.

## Information beyond Labels or Gestures

At present, very little is known about the nature of information provided by parents that extends beyond labeling or pointing. In a study of 12-, 15-, and 18-month-old children, DeLoache and DeMendoza (1987) found that 74% of the information provided by mothers while reading an alphabet book to their children was, in their words, "simple" (i.e., labels, sounds, or letter names). However, the amount of more "elaborated" information (including facts, dramatizations, and references to the child's experience) increased substantially across the ages studied (from 12% to 42%). Thus, even by 18 months, nearly half the information that children heard in this context extended beyond labeling. Interestingly, this was so even though parents were reading an alphabet book, which may not be ideally suited for eliciting such talk as it presumably provides little else beyond the pictured objects and the corresponding letters and words.

The amount of elaborated information that parents provide continues to increase beyond 18 months. For example, Adams and Bullock (1986, p. 187) found that parents of 3-year-olds provide categorical statements such as, "They [penguins] live at the South Pole and they swim and they catch fish." Callanan and Oakes (1992) found that parents of children as young as 3 years of age provide explanations prompted by children's questions regarding a range of biological, physical, and mental phenomena.

Callanan (1990) has examined directly the issue of what information about categories parents provide beyond labeling. In one study, parents were asked to teach a set of four basic-level and four superordinate-level concepts to their children (who ranged in age from 2-3 to 4-2), one concept at a time. In a second study, parents were asked to teach four subordinate- and four basic-level concepts to their children (who ranged in age from 2-0 to 4-5). For each concept to be taught, the mother was given a set of pictures of category instances that could be used at her discretion. The researcher provided no further information to parents regarding how to teach these concepts, with the goal of examining the kinds of strategies parents might ordinarily use with their children.

Callanan found that the information that parents provided varied with category level. Parents focused more on perceptual features and parts when teaching their children about basic- and subordinate-level categories and focused more on functions when teaching their children superordinate-level categories. Parents also tended to talk more about typical features than idiosyncratic features. These findings suggest that parental input may help children focus on features that are important to the category being discussed (see also Mervis & Mervis, 1988). More generally, parental input may help guide and limit the content of children's inferences (e.g., members of a basic-level category, such as *wrench*, tend to have similar perceptual features and parts; members of a superordinate-level category, such as *tool*, tend to have similar functions). Callanan also makes the interesting proposal that parental descriptions may help children learn, not just which features or kinds of features to associate with a particular category, but also which categories are coherent and can be expected to share many features. For example, when a parent describes vehicles as "things that move," the child may learn, not only that movement is typical of vehicles, but also that vehicles as a class have common properties.

In sum, little research has investigated parental input beyond labeling, but existing work suggests that parents focus on properties that are important for the category in question. These findings raise at least four additional questions that are fundamental to a broader understanding of the role of parental input: (1) How salient are taxonomic categories in a context that presents other kinds of information as well? (2) By what means do parents generalize information beyond individual instances? (3) Do parents distinguish between categories that support especially many rich inductions (e.g., animal species) and categories that are less richly structured (e.g., many artifact categories)? And, if so, how *explicitly* do they do so? (4) Finally, how do parents' gestures provide information beyond labeling?

## PRESENT STUDIES

The present set of studies is designed to examine the information children hear and see that extends beyond labeling, with a particular focus on information regarding categories. The picture-book-reading context, so prevalent in middle-class U.S. families, seems especially likely to elicit category-relevant information (Lucariello & Nelson, 1986). This task is also attractive in that it permits some control over the subject matter of conversations by means of custom-designed picture books.

We hypothesized that, if parental input contributes to children's understanding, it should do so in several ways. First, it should focus attention primarily on taxonomic categories as opposed to such other conceptual structures as individual objects, story scripts, or thematic relations between objects. Second, it should include general statements that emphasize commonalities among category members rather than idiosyncratic features of individuals. Finally, it should mention nonobvious properties, such as internal parts or appearance-reality conflicts, particularly those shown to be important in children's early reasoning about categories.

Furthermore, if input contributes to children's realization that not all categories exhibit rich structure, then such talk should be selective, focusing on categories that for adults are richly structured. Specifically, there should be domain differences in parental input, with more focus on categories, general statements, and nonobvious properties for richly structured categories. In what follows, we provide the outlines of what kinds of adult language and gestures would be expected if children were primarily deriving their knowledge about category structure from parental input.

### Attention to Categories as Opposed to Other Conceptual Structures

Richly structured categories tend to be "taxonomic" (groupings of like things) as opposed to "thematic" (groupings of things that interact) (see Markman, 1989). Although both thematic and taxonomic relations can transcend surface similarity (Mandler, Fivush, & Reznick, 1987), only taxonomic kinds permit vast numbers of inductive inferences (Markman, 1989; Waxman, 1990). Nonetheless, preschool children are highly attentive to thematic relations (Markman & Hutchinson, 1984; Nelson, 1977; Smiley & Brown, 1979; but see Blewitt & Toppino, 1991; Waxman & Namy, 1997). Surprisingly, to this point no data have been available regarding the relative frequency or salience of thematic and taxonomic relations in parental speech or gestures. If children's assumptions about richly structured categories depend on input, parents should focus special attention on taxonomic categories, as opposed to either (a) objects considered individually (this particular apple) or (b) nontaxonomic relations, such as perceptual similarity (e.g., a balloon and an orange) or thematic relations (e.g., a baby and a bottle).

### Generalizations about Category Members

Another way input could convey rich category structure is by conveying generalizations that hold across most or all category members. We focus on two kinds of generalizations: (a) generic statements (e.g., *Dogs bark, A giraffe is an animal*), which refer to a category as an abstract whole rather than referring to a specific individual (Carlson & Pelletier, 1995), and (b) statements explicitly referring to "all" category members (e.g., *All dogs bark, All giraffes are animals*), which are, from a logical perspective, the most direct and unambiguous in informing children about inductive potential.

### Domain-Specific and Nonobvious Properties

If rich category structure is explicit in the input that parents provide, parents would be expected to discuss nonobvious properties of the sorts that have been shown to be present in children's early reasoning about categories, particularly biological categories. Such properties would include *appearance-reality* distinctions (e.g., Flavell et al., 1983), which explicitly contrast what entities look like with what they really are; descriptions of animals' *insides,* as these are crucial to their identity and functioning (Backscheider, Coley, & Gutheil, 1991; Gelman, 1990; Gelman & Wellman, 1991); the natural, nonhuman *origins* of animals (Gelman & Kremer, 1991); and *causal explanations,* especially of domain-specific biological processes (Carey, 1985). *Teleology,* or the belief that living things exhibit properties because those properties confer some benefit on the individual possessing them, may be a distinctive feature of early naive biology (Keil, 1992; but see Kelemen, 1996) and thus would also be expected to be explicit in parental talk about living things. Likewise, parents might explicitly provide information about *self-initiated movements* of animals (Gelman & Gottfried, 1996; Mandler, 1992; Massey & Gelman, 1988) and *kinship,* particularly to explain inheritance and the importance of innate potential relative to environmental forces (Hirschfeld, 1996; Springer, 1992). Finally, parents might provide explicit information about *mental states* or *personality traits* (Bartsch & Wellman, 1995; Wellman, 1990). In sum, if children derive their appreciation for the importance of nonobvious properties from parental input, then parents can be expected to discuss such properties with children.

### Domain Differences

The issue of domain differentiation in input crosscuts the previous three sections. In order to examine how parents talk about richly structured categories, it is necessary to contrast such talk with input regarding categories that are not so structured. For this purpose, we chose to contrast animals (as richly structured) and artifacts (as less richly structured). Both animal and artifact categories exhibit clusters of correlated attributes. Thus, they do not represent an extreme contrast, as would comparing animals to a highly impoverished category—*red things,* for example. Nonetheless, the comparison is especially important for our purposes. As argued above, animals and artifacts differ with respect to such theory-laden properties as the kinds of inductions possible, the importance of nonobvious features, and potential for an essence (Keil, 1989; Markman, 1989). Moreover, unlike a starker contrast comparing animal categories with arbitrary categories (e.g., *red things*), the animal-artifact contrast allows us to unconfound other differences. Specifically, both kinds of categories are potentially equivalent in familiarity, thematic relatedness with other items, and object complexity.

Thus, we will compare how parents talk about animals with how they talk about artifacts. If parental input is informative regarding domain differences

13

in the degree to which categories are richly structured, then attention to categories as opposed to other conceptual structures, generalizations about category members, and emphasis on nonobvious properties should all be more pronounced for animal categories (as relatively more richly structured) than for artifact categories (as relatively less richly structured).

## Summary and Overview

To summarize, preschoolers show evidence of having richly structured categories in several conceptual domains. Furthermore, they appropriately limit the extent to which they assume that categories have this structure. Our goal was to explore the acquisition of these categories by looking at the kinds of information parents provide about category structure, beyond labeling (about which much is already known), through language and gestures. Specifically, we explored how parental input could convey to children that categories have inductive potential and capture nonobvious similarities and that categories differ in the degree to which they display this structure. Surprisingly little is known about parental input of this sort. However, an accurate account of conceptual development demands detailed characterization of the input available to children as well as the nature of the child's conceptual systems.

We examined these questions in three studies using a natural, picture-book-reading task (see Ninio & Bruner, 1978; Whitehurst, Arnold, Epstein, & Angell, 1994). We provided parents with the opportunity to talk and gesture about a variety of kinds of conceptual structures and contrasted speech and gestures regarding within-category similarities with speech and gestures regarding other conceptual structures (e.g., thematic links). We examined in detail information that would foster using categories to make inductive inferences or assume essences. Finally, we analyzed gestures to reveal information that may not be expressed in speech. Although our interest is in *parental* input, of the families we contacted only mothers chose to participate in the book-reading task. Therefore, we refer to participants as *mothers* rather than *parents*.

In Studies 1 and 3, mothers and their children were videotaped as they looked through picture books that we designed. These books enabled us to control several factors of interest, including familiarity of the pictures, similarity and thematic relations between pictures, and number of pictures per page. Most important, the books were designed to permit comparison of the extent to which mothers discussed different kinds of relations among the pictures and to compare input patterns for animal and artifact categories. In Study 2, participants were provided with commercially available, informational picture books, and mother-child pairs were videotaped while looking through and reading the books. The advantage to using commercially available books is that they set up a situation that is similar to actual interactions mothers and children have outside the laboratory.

## Age Comparisons

In this work, we focus on two age groups: 35-month-olds and 20-month-olds. Much of the work investigating richly structured categories has revealed important understandings by age 4, including inductive potential, essentialist beliefs, the importance of insides and other nonobvious properties, beliefs in inheritance, etc. By examining maternal speech to 35-month-olds, we can characterize the input preceding these achievements. Furthermore, researchers report that parents of 3-year-olds provide more semantic information than just labeling (Adams & Bullock, 1986). Thus, we should have an opportunity to see a variety of devices mothers employ when talking about category structure.

Although 35-month-olds are of primary interest, there are additional reasons for studying 20-month-olds. At least some initial assumptions about category structure are in place even before age 3. For example, 2½-year-olds treat categories as the basis of induction and accept anomalous category instances (Gelman & Coley, 1990; Gopnik & Meltzoff, 1997; Mandler & McDonough, 1996). Thus, it is important to see what kinds of input could precede these basic insights. At the same time, previous studies suggest that parents provide substantially less information when reading books to children younger than 3 years of age, focusing instead on simple labeling about the here and now (Adams & Bullock, 1986). Wheeler (1983) also found striking changes between 1½ and 3 years in the complexity and informativeness of maternal speech in joint book reading.

Although these differences suggest that important shifts in the complexity of input occur during the preschool years, the available literature does not focus on input regarding nonobvious properties, inductive potential, or the relative salience of category information. Our primary question with this younger group is what kind of input is possible with these simpler conversations. Do parents simply label the pictures without elaboration? To what extent do mothers focus on taxonomic categories when the input appears on the surface to be minimal? We chose to target 20-month-olds because they are considerably younger than our primary target group, 3-year-olds, yet old enough to engage in the task. By 20 months of age, children interact during book reading in a fairly mature way, by pointing at pictures and naming them (Murphy, 1978). By this age, children are no longer mouthing corners, scratching at the pictures as if to lift them off the page, or focusing on page turning (Murphy, 1978).

*Participant Sample*

These studies were designed to look at the kinds of information mothers provide in an information-rich, literacy-dense environment. The studies thus examine input provided by mothers who are, on the whole, highly articulate, literate, well educated, and comfortable reading to their children. An advantage to this approach is that it makes it easier for us to chart *how* and *when* mothers provide information regarding the rich structure of categories. Furthermore, to the extent that such mothers *refrain from* providing certain kinds of speech, we have even stronger evidence of what kinds of maternal statements are rare. The obvious disadvantage, and one that we take up again in Chapter VIII below, is that care must be taken in deciding which results from this select sample can be generalized to other cultures or even to others of different backgrounds within the United States.

*Data from Children*

In order to investigate the nature of the input to conceptual development, this *Monograph* focuses primarily on maternal speech and gesture. However, children's speech and gestures are also examined, in order to address the issue of who leads the topic and content of the conversations. Specifically, we can examine the extent to which children structure or determine the kinds of input they hear, what sorts of information children elicit or request from their mothers, and what sorts of information mothers provide independently. These issues can be addressed in two ways: By examining children's questions, we can see what information children explicitly request or elicit. And, by charting mismatches between maternal and children's speech (e.g., what they talk about and how), we can see ways that mothers provide a different focus of attention. For example, as will be seen in the chapters that follow, mothers focus on animals more than artifacts in certain ways. To the extent that children fail to show this pattern, it would suggest that the maternal pattern is mother led.

*Organization of the Remaining Chapters*

Chapter II provides detailed information regarding the participant sample and the methods of the three experiments as well as an overview of the database. Each of Chapters III–VII takes up a specific topic, using a different type of evidence, and presents relevant results from all three studies. Specifically, Chapter III addresses the question, How often do mothers focus attention on taxonomic categories as opposed to other conceptual structures (thematic categories and individual instances)? Chapter IV, How frequently do mothers convey category generalizations, and what are the most common linguistic devices for doing so? Chapter V, Do mothers explicitly mention such nonobvious, domain-specific properties as internal parts or category essences? Chapter VI, What gestures do mothers use to convey taxonomic categories? Chapter VII, How does maternal input about categories vary depending on category familiarity? Finally, Chapter VIII provides a general discussion of the findings in their entirety and their implications for the theoretical issues raised above.

# II. DESIGN, METHODS, AND DESCRIPTIVE OVERVIEW

The present *Monograph* reports findings from three separate studies, each examining maternal input about categories during a book-reading task. The studies differed from one another in two major respects: (*a*) Studies 1 and 2 were restricted to mothers of older children (mean age 35 months), whereas Study 3 was restricted to mothers of younger children (mean age 20 months); and (*b*) Studies 1 and 3 made use of specially prepared picture books that we created, whereas Study 2 made use of commercially available picture books. (For an overview of the design of the three studies, see Table 1.) In this chapter, we describe the participants, the materials (including the custom-designed picture books of Studies 1 and 3 and the commercially available picture books of Study 2), the procedures, and the transcription methods used for all three studies as well as an overview of the database.

## METHODS

### Participants

Participants were mother-child dyads, contacted from birth announcements in local newspapers, with equal numbers of boys and girls in each study. The participants in Study 1 included 16 dyads, with children (8 girls, 8 boys) ranging in age from 32 to 38 months (mean age 35 months). Participants in Study 2 included 14 dyads, with children (7 girls, 7 boys) ranging in age from 32 to 40 months (mean age 35 months). The participants in Study 3 were 16 dyads, with children (8 girls, 8 boys) ranging in age from 18 to 23 months (mean age 20 months). (For demographic information concerning the parents, see Table 2. For information regarding parents' level of reading activities and literacy, see Table 3.)

Several measures from maternal questionnaires (see our discussion of procedures below) validate our use of mothers in these studies as well as our focus on picture-book reading more generally. Mothers reported being the person who talked with their children the most or reported that they talked with their

## TABLE 1

OVERVIEW OF DESIGN

|  | Study 1 | Study 2 | Study 3 |
|---|---|---|---|
| Participants | 16 mother-child dyads | 14 mother-child dyads | 16 mother-child dyads |
| Child age range | 32–38 months | 32–40 months | 18–23 months |
| Child mean age | 35 months | 35 months | 20 months |
| Books | Custom designed | Commercial | Custom designed |
| Domain of books | Animals, artifacts | Farm animals, trucks | Animals, artifacts |
| No. of books per dyad | 2 | 2 | 1 |

## TABLE 2

DEMOGRAPHIC DATA REGARDING PARENTS IN STUDIES 1, 2, AND 3

|  | Study 1 | Study 2 | Study 3 |
|---|---|---|---|
| Percentage of respondents who are female | 100 | 100 | 94[a] |
| Age range of mothers (%): | | | |
| 25–29 years | 6 | 43 | 25 |
| 30–34 years | 31 | 29 | 31 |
| 35–39 years | 56 | 29 | 31 |
| 40–44 years | 6 | 0 | 6 |
| 45–49 years | 0 | 0 | 6 |
| Mother's highest level of schooling (%): | | | |
| Some college | 19 | 29 | 19 |
| College degree | 25 | 43 | 25 |
| Postcollege education | 56 | 29 | 56 |
| Spouse's age (%): | | | |
| 25–29 years | 6 | 36 | 12.5 |
| 30–34 years | 37.5 | 35 | 19 |
| 35–39 years | 44 | 14 | 25 |
| 40–44 years | 12.5 | 0 | 18 |
| 45–49 years | 0 | 0 | 12.5 |
| 50 years or older | 0 | 7 | 0 |
| Spouse's highest level of schooling (%): | | | |
| Some college | 12.5 | 21 | 19 |
| College degree | 31 | 36 | 19 |
| Postcollege education | 56 | 36 | 50 |
| Number of siblings (%): | | | |
| None | 18 | 14 | 50 |
| One | 75 | 71 | 37.5 |
| Two or more | 6 | 14 | 12.5 |

NOTE.—Data were obtained from parental questionnaires.

[a] For one family, the mother participated in the book-reading session, and the father filled out the questionnaire.

TABLE 3

Parental[a] Responses to Questionnaire regarding Reading and Literacy, from Studies 1, 2, and 3

| Question/Response | Study 1 | Study 2 | Study 3 |
|---|---|---|---|
| Who talks to the child the most? (%): | | | |
| Mother | 69 | 93 | 88 |
| Mother and other | 19 | 7 | 6 |
| Other | 12 | 0 | 6 |
| Who plays with the child the most? (%): | | | |
| Mother | 31 | 57 | 38 |
| Father | 25 | 7 | 12 |
| Mother and father | 12 | 14 | 6 |
| Other | 31 | 21 | 44 |
| Who reads to the child the most? (%): | | | |
| Mother | 44 | 79 | 81 |
| Father | 25 | 0 | 0 |
| Mother and father | 25 | 21 | 13 |
| Other | 6 | 0 | 6 |
| How many times per month does the child go to the library? | 1.3 | .8 | 2.3 |
| How many books does your child have at home? | 65.8 | 71.2 | 60.1 |
| How old [in months] was your child when you began to read to him/her? | 7.9 | 6.6 | 3.7 |
| How many times a week do you read to your child? | 12.5 | 10.5 | 13.8 |
| How long [in minutes] does each reading session last? | 19.9 | 21.1 | 11.8 |
| Who initiates the reading session? (%): | | | |
| Mother | 25 | 14 | 37.5 |
| Child | 62.5 | 50 | 25 |
| Other | 12.5 | 36 | 37.5 |
| Do you read to the child individually or with others? (%): | | | |
| Individually | 81 | 64 | 69 |
| With others | 19 | 36 | 31 |
| When do you read to the child? (%): | | | |
| Bedtime only | 56 | 43 | 29 |
| Morning and bedtime | 12 | 36 | 43 |
| Other | 32 | 21 | 28 |
| What happens when you and your child look at books together? (%): | | | |
| Mother asks questions, child answers them | 12.5 | 7 | 44 |
| Child asks questions, mother answers them | 19 | 7 | 0 |
| Share asking and answering questions | 50 | 50 | 25 |
| Child listens to reading, neither asks questions | 6 | 7 | 0 |
| Depends on book | 12.5 | 29 | 31 |
| Why is reading important for the child? (ranking from 1 = most important to 7 = least important): | | | |
| Providing interaction | 2.5 | 2.5 | 2.1 |
| Improving thinking | 2.9 | 2.8 | 2.9 |
| Improving speaking | 3.9 | 4.2 | 2.9 |
| Providing information | 3.4 | 4.4 | 4.2 |
| Entertainment | 4.4 | 4.1 | 4.4 |
| Improving reading | 4.7 | 4.4 | 5.4 |
| Communicating values | 4.9 | 5.7 | 5.3 |
| How many hours per week do you read? | 9.4 | 6.6 | 9.9 |

TABLE 3 (*Continued*)

| Question/Response | Study 1 | Study 2 | Study 3 |
|---|---|---|---|
| How many hours a week does spouse read? ............. | 12.1 | 12.2 | 11.4 |
| Reasons for reading (ranking from 1 = most important to 5 = least important): | | | |
| Obtaining information ............................ | 2.0 | 1.6 | 1.7 |
| Entertainment/relaxation ......................... | 1.7 | 2.1 | 1.9 |
| Improving thinking ............................... | 2.9 | 2.7 | 2.3 |
| Improving speaking ............................... | 4.1 | 4.2 | 4.3 |
| Improving reading ................................ | 4.3 | 4.4 | 4.6 |
| Reasons for spouse's reading (ranking from 1 = most important to 5 = least important): | | | |
| Obtaining information ............................ | 1.9 | 1.3 | 1.6 |
| Entertainment/relaxation ......................... | 1.9 | 2.9 | 1.7 |
| Improving thinking ............................... | 2.8 | 2.5 | 2.8 |
| Improving speaking ............................... | 3.9 | 4.1 | 4.3 |
| Improving reading ................................ | 4.5 | 4.2 | 4.6 |
| Number of newspapers or magazines ................... | 6.6 | 4.8 | 7.1 |

[a] For all but one family, mothers filled out the questionnaire.

children as often as fathers did. Mothers also reported being the person who read most often with their children or reported reading with their children as often as fathers. All mothers reported having begun reading to their child prior to the start of the study and, at the time of their participation in the study, were reading to their children over 10 times per week on average.

Demographically, the participant samples in all three studies were very similar. The mothers were highly educated: all had at least a high school diploma, and the majority had a college degree and/or postcollege education. Mothers of the older children (Studies 1 and 2) reported that they began reading to their children at a significantly older age than did mothers of the younger children (Study 3) ($F[2, 43] = 3.9$, $p < .05$). They also reported reading for significantly longer periods of time per reading session than the mothers of the younger children did ($F[2, 43] = 5.2$, $p < .01$). Mothers of the younger children (Study 3) reported reading to improve their own thinking more often than mothers of the older children in Study 1 ($F[2, 43] = 4.1$, $p < .05$). Spouses of mothers in Study 2 were rated as somewhat less likely to read for entertainment or relaxation than spouses in the other two studies ($F[2, 43] = 5.9$, $p < .01$). Otherwise, there were no significant differences among the samples.

### Materials: Studies 1 and 3 (Custom-Designed Picture Books)

For Studies 1 and 3, we created special picture books—one animal book (*Animals Friends*) and one artifact book (*Things in Our World*)—that permitted control over the content and structure of each page, with the aim of providing mothers with the opportunity to discuss category structure in a variety of ways. Each book was composed of nine $8\frac{1}{2} \times 11$-inch pages bound between covers. Each page included color pictures of four objects that were integrated into a scene (e.g., a farm scene, a beach scene, a living-room scene). The objects were selected so that two belonged to the same basic-level ("target") category (e.g., two different horses), a third belonged to a closely contrasting category (e.g., a zebra), and the fourth was thematically related in some way to the target (e.g., a barn). The four pictures were located roughly in each of the four quadrants of the page. Each picture was labeled (e.g., a horse had the word *horse* printed just below it).[3] There were two versions of each book, differing only in page order (random, in both cases). The pictures/labels are listed in Table 4, along with maternal familiarity ratings (described in more detail later in this section). Figure 1 provides schematic drawings of two sample pages (one animal, one artifact). (Note that the actual pages provided more detail and were in full color.)

Each page was designed with three purposes in mind. First, by including two exemplars of each target category as well as a contrasting exemplar and a thematic associate, we hoped to increase the contexts in which it would be appropriate for mothers to talk about category structure. That is, mothers would have the opportunity to talk about category structure in a variety of ways. For example, they could label pictures, note similarity among category members, note dissimilarity between contrasting-category members, or discuss thematic relations. By providing mothers with books that enabled them to talk about categories in different ways, we hoped to gather a rich data set that included statements that might otherwise be difficult to sample.

Second, and relatedly, the items were designed to foster discussion of how and why taxonomic category membership and perceptual similarity can come into conflict. For example, one page included eels and snakes, which are highly similar; another page included a Snoopy-phone, which looks like Snoopy but is actually a telephone. Items such as these were chosen to encourage more explicit maternal speech regarding how appearances can be deceiving and nonobvious properties can be important.

Third, we arranged each page as we did in order to assess the *relative* frequency with which mothers talk specifically about taxonomic relations, as compared to thematic or similarity relations (both of which have been proposed to be highly salient relations to young children; Markman & Hutchin-

[3] Providing printed labels for each picture may have encouraged mothers to talk more about taxonomic similarity than they might otherwise have. However, a comparison with the data from Study 2 suggests that this was not the case. Furthermore, the labels were necessary in order to ensure that mothers were certain of the identity of all the pictures, some of which were relatively unfamiliar (e.g., eel).

TABLE 4

CONTENT OF BOOKS USED IN STUDIES 1 AND 3, BY PAGE, WITH MATERNAL FAMILIARITY RATINGS

| Target 1 | Target 2 | Contrast | Thematic | Familiarity[a,b] | Familiarity[a,c] |
|---|---|---|---|---|---|
| | | ANIMALS | | | |
| Horse | Horse | Zebra | Barn | 1.12 (.34) | 1.53 (.61) |
| Squirrel | Squirrel | Chipmunk | Acorns | 1.31 (.43) | 1.90 (.41) |
| Cat | Cat | Raccoon | Ball of yarn | 1.35 (.46) | 1.80 (.43) |
| Seal | Seal | Walrus | Ball | 1.40 (.37) | 2.09 (.39) |
| Bat | Bat | Bird | Cave | 1.61 (.48) | 2.20 (.27) |
| Crab | Crab | Lobster | Pail | 1.63 (.56) | 2.50 (.37) |
| Dolphin | Dolphin | Shark | Hoop | 1.69 (.59) | 2.59 (.53) |
| Eel | Eel | Snake | Seaweed | 2.22 (.45) | 2.63 (.30) |
| Anteater | Anteater | Aardvark | Anthill | 2.55 (.55) | 2.95 (.14) |
| | | ARTIFACTS | | | |
| Desk | Desk | Table | Chair | 1.12 (.25) | 1.63 (.39) |
| Book | Book | Magazine | Bookcase | 1.14 (.31) | 1.64 (.38) |
| Car-clock | Clock | Toy car | Batteries | 1.45 (.25) | 2.15 (.35) |
| Boot-car | Car | Boot | Traffic light | 1.57 (.15) | 2.38 (.23) |
| Sneaker | Sneaker | Thongs | Socks | 1.68 (.43) | 2.15 (.30) |
| Snoopy-phone | Telephone | Snoopy doll | Notepad | 1.72 (.42) | 2.34 (.32) |
| Wok | Wok | Pot | Vegetables | 1.92 (.39) | 2.42 (.40) |
| Safe | Safe | Refrigerator[d] | Money[d] | 2.08 (.38) | 2.47 (.26) |
| Tongs | Tongs | Compass | Ice | 2.17 (.35) | 2.63 (.21) |

NOTE.—Each row represents a particular page (e.g., horse, horse, zebra, and barn were all on a single page). Standard deviations are given in parentheses.

[a] Composite scores, averaged across all four pictures per page. These mean ratings are based on a three-point scale: 1 = the child has spontaneously said the word before; 2 = the child understands the word but has never said it before; 3 = the child does not know the word.

[b] Study 1 mothers.

[c] Study 3 mothers.

[d] Refrigerator and money were inadvertently left off the parental questionnaire. These values wre interpolated from children's naming scores (see the text).

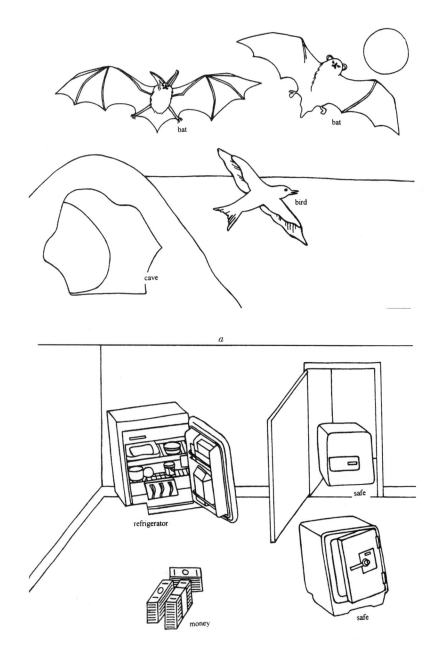

FIGURE 1.—Schematic drawings of sample pages, Studies 1 and 3. (Actual pages were in full color.)

son, 1984; Smith, 1989), when all three kinds of relations are available in the stimulus materials. Although information relayed when discussing taxonomic relations is undoubtedly also relevant to discussions of thematic and similarity relations, it is also of interest to assess the relative frequency with which each of these kinds of relations is discussed.

### Pretest Data

In order to control as much as possible for perceptual similarity, thematic relatedness, and familiarity across domains, we created 24 scenes that we pretested with adults ($N = 12$) and then compared to children's naming and match-to-sample data. From this initial set, 18 scenes (9 animal and 9 artifact) were selected for use in the study. The final scenes were chosen on the basis of adult ratings, which provided the most direct measure of similarity and thematic relatedness. For perceptual similarity judgments, adult participants rated pairs of pictures on each page on a scale ranging from 1 ("not at all similar") to 7 ("extremely similar"). In order to assess the strength of the thematic associations, adult participants rated pairs of pictures on a scale ranging from 1 ("not at all related") to 7 ("extremely related"). For both sets of judgments, labels for the pictures were provided. For each page of the picture book, participants made three similarity ratings (all pairwise comparisons excluding the thematic associate) and three thematic ratings (the thematic associate paired with each of the other three pictures). For example, similarity ratings for the bat page involved the two bats, the first bat and the bird, and the second bat and the bird. Thematic ratings for the bat page involved the cave and the first bat, the cave and the second bat, and the cave and the bird (see Figure 1).

On the basis of the adult ratings, the final scenes were selected with four goals in mind:

    *a*) to include pictures of contrasting categories that were each relatively similar in appearance to at least one of the pictures of same-category instances (e.g., a zebra and a horse);
    *b*) to include a thematic associate that was highly related to at least one of the same-category pictures and that was (on average) more highly related to the same-category pictures than to the contrasting category (e.g., the barn should be highly related to at least one of the horses and should be more highly related to the horses than to the zebra);
    *c*) to ensure that the animal sets were as comparable as possible to the artifact sets, with respect to perceptual similarity; and
    *d*) to ensure that the animal sets were as comparable as possible to the artifact sets, with respect to thematic relatedness.

25

As reported in the Appendix, the final scenes met three of the four goals. The one exception concerned perceptual similarity (goal *c*), as the animal sets were overall more similar than the artifact sets. In later chapters, we control for this domain difference by including supplementary analyses that examine only those animal and artifact scenes that overlap in similarity.

### Familiarity Ratings

Familiarity ratings, obtained from maternal questionnaires (see below), were based on mothers' assessments of children's knowledge of the words used in the books (see Table 4). Specifically, mothers were asked to judge, for each word, whether their child (*a*) had spontaneously said the word before, (*b*) understood the word but had never said it, or (*c*) did not know the word. Because the words *refrigerator* and *money* were accidentally omitted from the questionnaire, scores for these words were interpolated on the basis of the relative familiarity of these words in children's naming data. The scores presented in Table 4 are *composite* scores for each page, based on the familiarity ratings for each of the four pictures per page (e.g., horse$_1$ + horse$_2$ + zebra + barn), divided by four. When the two target-category instances received the same word (as in 15 of the 18 pages), we simply double weighted the rating for that word. Ratings could range from 1 (most familiar) to 3 (least familiar). For the older children (Study 1), the mean familiarity rating for both animals and artifacts was 1.65. For the younger children (Study 3), the mean familiarity rating for animals was 2.24, and that for artifacts was 2.20. At both age groups, familiarity ratings for animals did not differ significantly from familiarity ratings for artifacts. Familiarity ratings across the two samples (Studies 1 and 3) correlated .80 (above chance, $p < .01$).

### Children's Naming

Data from a separate group of children ($N = 14$, ages 33–39 months, mean age 36 months) were gathered in order to obtain converging evidence regarding the familiarity of items. Children were simply asked to name all the pictures from both books. None of these children participated in any other aspect of this research. In order to make the task enjoyable to the children, they were introduced to an "alien" stuffed toy and asked to name the pictures for him in order to help him learn what we call things.

Children were fairly equally accurate in their ability to identify the pictures for animals and artifacts ($M$'s = 16.14 and 17.36 correct, respectively, of 36 possible, N.S.). When focusing on children's exact matches to the labels that mothers were asked to rate, a correlation of .67 ($p < .01$) was obtained between the children's naming data and the maternal ratings of familiarity. The maternal ratings were based on an $N$ of 30, combining participants from Studies 1 and 3 (all of whom rated the same set of words); the correlations were conducted on a word-by-word basis ($N = 55$ words). This result indicates that the items that children found easiest to name tended to be items that mothers reported their own children knew best. More specifically, these data suggest that familiarity ratings provided by mothers for their own children are significantly related to naming data provided by an independent sample of children. Thus, the maternal familiarity ratings can be viewed as providing a valid measure of children's word knowledge.

The naming data also indicate that children found the category membership of the pictures somewhat misleading. On 38% of the picture sets, they used the same label for the target- and the contrasting-category instances. Conversely, on 39% of the picture sets, they used different labels for the target- and the same-category instances.

### Children's Match to Sample

Although the naming data suggest that children regularly misclassify the pictures, this result could reflect vocabulary limitations. We therefore also included a match-to-sample task in order to provide converging evidence on the issue of how often children are misled regarding the category membership of the items. Because the match-to-sample task is more demanding than the naming task, participants were older (ages 42–53 months, mean age 47 months, $N = 57$).

None of the children who participated in the match-to-sample tasks had participated in other aspects of this project. We predicted that children would often group the target-category instance with the contrasting-category instance (e.g., horse and zebra), as such a pattern would confirm that the taxonomic relations were sometimes unclear to the children. We expected that such confusions would encourage mothers to explain the taxonomic structure of the items to their children.

Because differing instructions are known to influence children's sorting (e.g., Deák & Bauer, 1995; Mandler & Bauer, 1988; Markman & Hutchinson, 1984; Smiley & Brown, 1979; Vosniadou & Ortony, 1986; Waxman & Gelman, 1986; Waxman & Kosowski, 1990), we included two kinds of instructions: neutral ("Which one of these [pointing to remaining three pictures] goes best with this one [pointing to target]?") and taxonomically biased ("Which one of these [pointing to remaining three pictures] has the same kinds of stuff inside as this one [pointing to target]?"). Thus, the design was a 2 (instructions: goes with, insides) × 2 (domain: animals, artifacts) study, with type

27

of instructions as a between-subjects factor and domain as a within-subject factor.

Details of the procedure and results are provided in the Appendix. The findings indicate that, when the experimenter provided no labels and asked children to sort the pictures, participants typically chose either the same-category pictures (52% of choices) or the contrasting-category pictures (38% of choices). This was so whether the instructions were neutral ("goes with") or taxonomically biased ("same insides"). Moreover, those items on which children chose the target-category member least often and the contrasting-category member most often were the same items on which children in the naming task tended to err (for details, see the Appendix). This suggests that children chose the contrasting-category members in the belief that they were of the same category as the target pictures. Altogether, then, with the present items children were focused primarily on what they thought were same-category relations but what were in fact either same-category or contrasting-category relations. Thus, as predicted, the actual category membership of these items often conflicts with children's expectations.

Further, in order to test whether children's errors are indeed due to confusion regarding the identity of the items rather than an inability or aversion to sort taxonomically, we also included a second study in which all pictures were labeled before children sorted. Labeling the pictures should provide children with the information they need to sort taxonomically if they understand that this is what the task calls for. When the experimenter labeled the pictures, children made more same-category choices than they did in the previous study, when no labels were provided (73% and 52%, respectively). Thus, when explicitly told the category membership of the items, children generally preferred to sort on that basis. This again confirms the interpretation that children understood that the task called for taxonomic groupings and that their difficulty when no labels were provided reflected difficulties classifying these pictures rather than lack of understanding of the task. For example, when children to whom no labels were provided grouped an eel with a snake, they evidently did so because they thought that both items were snakes rather than because they thought that the experimenter wanted a grouping based on similarity.

An interesting side point is that, when no labels were provided, the "insides" wording yielded a small but significant difference in performance compared with that produced by the "goes with" wording. Specifically, children were less likely to select the thematic associate when asked to choose the item with the same insides as the target. This suggests that children may assume that taxonomic categories are more likely than thematic groupings to capture shared internal parts.

*Summary*

The custom-designed animal and artifact picture books contained a number of scenes, each of which depicted objects that were related perceptually, taxonomically, and thematically. Thus, the books provided readers with the opportunity to infer a variety of relations among objects for potential discussion. The structure of each page (including number and placement of pictures, number and level of taxonomic relations, number of contrasting-category relations, and number of thematic relations) was identical for animals and artifacts. Judged on the basis of data obtained independently from other adults and children, the animal and artifact books were equivalent with respect to familiarity of pictures and strength of thematic relations among pictures. Although animal and artifact pictures were roughly comparable with respect to perceptual similarity, animal pictures were rated as significantly more similar to each other overall than were artifacts, a finding that we take into account in subsequent analyses. Finally, naming and match-to-sample data from children suggest that children frequently confused target- and contrasting-category members, indicating that our attempts to select perceptually similar target and contrasting categories were successful.

*Materials: Study 2 (Commercially Available Picture Books)*

The materials for Study 2 were two commercially available picture books from the Random House Pictureback series—*Farm Animals* (Helweg, 1978) and *The Truck Book* (McNaught, 1978). The books were comparable to the custom-designed books and to one another in length (each was 15 pages) and format (each page included several pictures set into a scene). In addition, both books included text that provided information but no fictional story line, and both were targeted to the same age level. *The Truck Book* included pictures of and information about trucks, buses, campers, tractors, vans, trailers, and more. *Farm Animals* included pictures of and information about chickens, cows, goats, turkeys, horses, donkeys, cats, rabbits, geese, pigs, ducks, sheep, dogs, and more.

*Procedure (Studies 1–3)*

*Questionnaire*

Following the book-reading session, each mother received a questionnaire that assessed the degree of literacy in the home, the mothers' reading habits, and their beliefs about the value of reading to their children. It also included a set of questions regarding the parents' age and level of schooling and the number and ages of the target child's siblings. As mentioned previously, mothers also rated their child's familiarity with the labels used in all four of the books. The questionnaire took about 15–20 minutes to complete.

### Book-Reading Task

For the study proper, each mother-child dyad was escorted to a carpeted laboratory playroom that was comfortably furnished with a couch, a low table, and some cabinets, and both mother and child were seated on the couch. The mothers were told that the study concerned how parents and children look at books together. They were instructed to look through each book as they normally would at home. Our only special request was that the mothers try to look at every page in the books. Mothers of older children (Studies 1 and 2) looked through two books each, one at a time. The order of the books (e.g., animals or artifacts first) was counterbalanced across participants. Mothers of younger children (Study 3) looked through only one book each, as pilot testing revealed that children became restless after just one book. Eight mother-child pairs received the animal book, and eight received the artifact book.

All interactions were videotaped (with mothers' prior permission) through a one-way mirror. Separate audio input was provided by two microphones in the ceiling of the playroom. The angle of the videocamera was above and to the side of the participants and typically allowed coders to see each page clearly.

### Transcriptions

Each videotaped session was viewed by one of seven coders, who transcribed the speech produced by both mother and child. The transcribers began recording when the book was opened to the first page. Speech concerning the covers and (in Study 2) the title pages of the books was omitted because these sections were ignored by some of the dyads. Intelligible utterances were transcribed verbatim; unintelligible utterances were also noted. The transcriptions of Study 2 sessions did not, however, fully record mothers when they were reading from the text, simply noting the first and last few words of those portions of the text that were read aloud. All the transcriptions were checked against the videotape of the session by one of eight second coders. Disagreements were rare, and those that occurred were resolved through discussion.

Next, two coders (one of whom had not made any of the transcriptions) together reviewed the transcripts, while viewing the videotapes, to mark utterance units and provide a final check of accuracy. Utterances were defined as continuous units of conversation so identified according to content and intonational contour. *Continuous* was defined as being free of pauses, full stops, or interjections (e.g., interruptions from the second party). As such, utterances consisted of sentences, phrases, or even words if they were pronounced with final pitch (rising or falling intonation).

Special attention was given to utterances lacking clear boundaries. In particular, for cases in which intonation and pausing would have conflicted with one another with regard to deciding where to place an utterance break, the intonational cues were used instead of pausing. For run-on sentences, often characterized by a change of subject, the speech was divided into two or more utterances (Snow, 1972). Finally, stylistic features such as "filler" words (*OK, and, right, look, yeah*) and tag questions were combined with adjacent speech segments unless content and phonetic cues indicated that they were clearly distinct. This guideline was adopted to avoid extreme estimates of total number of utterances for participants who use these features often.

## DESCRIPTIVE OVERVIEW

### Coding

We identified all utterances that were to be discarded, including those providing procedural information (e.g., "Turn the page"), off-task utterances (e.g., "Put that down, honey"), those simply reading the text (Study 2), and those that could not be interpreted (e.g., those that were unintelligible, nonsensical, or nonverbal). All utterances that were not discarded are referred to as *coded utterances*. For the mean numbers of coded utterances per study, see Table 5.

Each transcript was coded by one of two coders, who classified each utter-

TABLE 5

MEAN NUMBER OF CODED UTTERANCES, BY STUDY

|  | MOTHERS | | CHILDREN | |
|---|---|---|---|---|
|  | Animals | Artifacts | Animals | Artifacts |
| Study 1 | 101.00 | 88.19 | 50.56 | 45.25 |
|  | (52.05) | (33.06) | (22.64) | (15.98) |
| Study 2 | 77.86 | 101.29 | 45.21 | 49.71 |
|  | (37.33) | (42.08) | (26.34) | (18.59) |
| Study 3 | 92.25 | 75.88 | 27.50 | 15.13 |
|  | (28.61) | (10.12) | (18.53) | (10.62) |

NOTE.—Standard deviations are given in parentheses.

ance with respect to four dimensions: label, information, question, and/or response. Because none of these coding categories excluded any other, utterances could receive multiple codes (e.g., label and information; question and response). However, each utterance received no more than one example of any code (e.g., an utterance could have no more than one "information" code).

*Questions* were any interrogatives, including tag questions. *Responses* included any reply to a directly preceding utterance by another person, including the repetition of that utterance:

> Child: Bird.
> Mother: A bird, yeah.

*Labels* were considered to be any utterances including a noun, such as labels for a whole object, part of an object, a place, a kind of substance, or a specific person, but not names of events, pronouns, or labels irrelevant to the book (e.g., the child's name). *Information* referred to utterances that expressed any information beyond labeling, including information about properties, function, behavior, familiarity, counting, etc. (e.g., "Remember we had a Christmas book with the bats living in the cave?"). Questions were not counted as informational unless (*a*) the utterance contained a tag question and the first phrase conveyed information (e.g., "No, that doesn't go on your feet, does it?") or (*b*) there was information in the question that the response could not negate (e.g., "Who do we talk to on the phone?" presupposes that we talk to someone on the phone).

Agreement was calculated by having both coders code a randomly chosen subset of the transcripts—four transcripts from Study 1, three from Study 2, and six from Study 3. Agreement—calculated as present or absent for each utterance—was considered present only when both coders agreed on all the descriptive codes for a given utterance (including whether it was to be discarded or coded). Agreement ranged from 83% (Study 3) to 88% (Study 2). Disagreements were resolved through discussion.

## Results

Table 6 shows the percentage of labels, informational utterances, questions, and responses, for both mothers and children, in all three studies. Because each utterance could be coded in multiple ways, the columns total to more than 100%. Of special interest is the fact that a sizable portion of the transcripts (over 30% of mothers' utterances in each study) included information beyond labeling. Consistent with past research, mothers asked more questions than children, and children gave proportionately more responses

TABLE 6

DESCRIPTIVE INFORMATION, AS MEAN NUMBER PER 100 CODED UTTERANCES

| | MOTHERS | | CHILDREN | |
|---|---|---|---|---|
| | Animals | Artifacts | Animals | Artifacts |
| Study 1: | | | | |
| Labels ............... | 63.17[a] | 56.62 | 44.09 | 46.58[a] |
| | (9.96) | (11.76) | (13.56) | (15.79) |
| Information .......... | 40.22 | 35.02 | 20.60 | 20.41 |
| | (11.36) | (10.93) | (8.52) | (11.36) |
| Questions ............ | 32.46 | 40.84 | 24.23 | 19.03 |
| | (11.15) | (16.52) | (14.66) | (15.98) |
| Responses ............ | 36.68 | 37.82 | 65.84 | 67.39 |
| | (15.68) | (15.59) | (19.13) | (19.08) |
| Study 2: | | | | |
| Labels ............... | 55.44 | 64.10 | 39.46 | 34.47 |
| | (5.77) | (9.72) | (19.10) | (13.79) |
| Information .......... | 39.89 | 43.10[b] | 30.90[b] | 20.97 |
| | (12.44) | (8.13) | (13.39) | (13.70) |
| Questions ............ | 40.71 | 31.56 | 20.39 | 27.42 |
| | (13.59) | (11.97) | (17.42) | (19.86) |
| Responses ............ | 33.55 | 30.08 | 58.07 | 54.49 |
| | (11.45) | (8.86) | (13.79) | (17.72) |
| Study 3: | | | | |
| Labels ............... | 67.42 | 59.53 | 52.71 | 61.56 |
| | (10.31) | (6.38) | (19.24) | (29.43) |
| Information .......... | 35.81 | 29.05 | 22.54 | 12.99 |
| | (10.91) | (7.22) | (13.52) | (13.11) |
| Questions ............ | 37.71 | 45.00 | 12.99 | 7.91 |
| | (11.17) | (11.21) | (11.60) | (13.41) |
| Responses ............ | 21.08 | 22.00 | 73.10 | 67.96 |
| | (10.53) | (8.56) | (13.77) | (31.65) |

NOTE.—Because each utterance could be coded in more than one way, columns total to more than 100%. Standard deviations are given in parentheses.

[a] Value for Study 1 is significantly higher than corresponding value for Study 2.

[b] Value for Study 2 is significantly higher than corresponding value for Study 1.

than mothers (Hirsh-Pasek & Treiman, 1982; Newport, Gleitman, & Gleitman, 1977). Neither the proportion of responses nor the mean total number of coded utterances differed between dyads reading the animal book and those reading the artifact book. However, in Study 1, mothers provided significantly higher proportions of labels, information, and utterances that were *not* questions (all $t$'s[15] > 2.3, all $p$'s < .05) when reading the animal book than when reading the artifact book.

We compared the data from Study 2 with those from Study 1 in order to gauge the extent to which the custom-designed books differed from the commercially available books in the sorts of conversational exchanges they elicited. In other words, we wished to know whether the custom-designed books were biasing the kind of input children received and, if so, how. On these comparisons, we found that, overall, talk about the two sets of books is comparable (as can be seen in Table 6), although a few differences arose. Mothers provided more labels when reading the custom-designed animal book than when reading the commercial animal book ($t[28]$ = 2.59, $p$ < .02). Likewise, children provided more labels for the custom-designed artifact book than for the commercial artifact book ($t[28]$ = 2.62, $p$ < .02). Conversely, children provided more informational statements for the commercial animal book than for the custom-designed animal book ($t[28]$ = 2.55, $p$ < .02), and mothers provided more informational statements for the commercial artifact book than for the custom-designed artifact book ($t[28]$ = 2.30, $p$ < .05). The finding that informational statements were somewhat more frequent for the commercial books suggests that our specially prepared books were not artificially inflating the amount of informational speech that children hear. None of the other comparisons were significant.

Comparing the data from Study 3 with those from Study 1, we found that, overall, younger children asked fewer questions and mothers of younger children provided fewer responses. Otherwise, the overall patterns of speech were quite similar.

## SUMMARY

Studies 1–3 were designed to provide converging evidence regarding early maternal input to children's category development, using two different sets of books, and two different age groups, but otherwise identical testing conditions and procedures. Maternal speech during picture-book reading contained a high proportion of verbal information beyond labeling, ranging from 32% of maternal utterances in speech to 20-month-olds to 35%–43% of maternal utterances in speech to 35-month-olds. The custom-designed picture books (used in Studies 1 and 3) are comparable to the commercial picture books (used in Study 2) in the amount of information they elicit from mothers. Thus, we can infer that the custom-designed books evoke a representative sample of maternal speech. In the following chapters, we look more closely at the nature of this input, examining maternal focus on taxonomic categories, category generalizations, nonobvious and domain-specific properties, and gestures.

# III. TAXONOMIC VERSUS THEMATIC LANGUAGE

As discussed in Chapter I, taxonomic categories provide a powerful means of organizing information about the world. One potentially crucial function of maternal input could be to convey the importance of taxonomic relations among objects. However, there exist other kinds of salient and ecologically significant relations among objects. Objects may be perceptually similar without belonging to the same basic-level taxonomic category (e.g., *horses* and *zebras, snakes* and *eels*). Objects also share thematic links with other objects (e.g., *horses* eat *hay,* live in *barns,* are fitted with *saddles,* and are ridden by *people,* all of which represent thematic links among different basic-level kinds). Thus, preschool children are simultaneously learning a variety of relations among objects. Does maternal input tend to emphasize one type of relation over another?

We predicted that, if maternal input contributes to children's understanding of richly structured categories, mothers would produce many taxonomic relations, especially for the animal domain. To assess the relative focus on taxonomic categories as opposed to other kinds of groupings (i.e., thematic, similarity), we examined relational statements (*relations*), defined as statements or series of statements in which the mother or the child links two or more items in some way, for example, "It's about the same color as this cat, but that's a raccoon."

As a comparison to relations, we also examined statements about individual objects. Whereas relations imply some kind of category or grouping, statements about individuals need not entail any categorization (beyond that needed to apply a label appropriately). If the two kinds of statements (relations and individual objects) yield the same patterns of results, it would suggest that maternal input about categories reduces to maternal input regarding the individual objects that constitute the categories. Such a finding would provide no evidence that mothers are focusing on category structure in their input to young children. In contrast, qualitative differences in maternal speech about relations as opposed to single objects would suggest, first, that input about categories extends beyond mere descriptions of individuals and, further, that mothers are conveying information about category structure.

In addition to studying maternal input, which was of primary interest, we performed a secondary set of analyses using the data from children. Specifically, we focused on (*a*) children's questions, to determine what sorts of information children elicited from their mothers, and (*b*) children's relations, to examine mother-child mismatches.

## CODING

Each transcript was coded by one of two coders, who examined (*a*) the *content* of relations and single-object statements (all three studies) and (*b*) which *pictures* were the focus of relations and single-object statements (Studies 1 and 3 only). All examples provided below are taken from actual transcripts.

### Content of Relations

The *content* of relational statements included taxonomic information (including basic, subordinate, and superordinate levels), thematic information, similarity information, and other information. *Taxonomic* refers to shared membership in some category, including explicitly labeling objects with the same name or more generally mentioning that they have the same name (e.g., "That's a desk. That's a desk, too," "These have the same name"). Each taxonomic relation was coded as superordinate (*animal, furniture*), basic (*cat, desk*), or subordinate (*baby kitten, tennis shoe/sneaker*) level. For *The Truck Book*, compound nouns that included a basic-level name as the head noun (e.g., *ice-cream truck, fire truck, lumber truck, camper van*) were counted as subordinate level relations, whereas other names were considered basic level (e.g., *camper, bus, truck, trailer*) or superordinate level (e.g., *heavy machinery*). *Thematic* involved relating objects via a common theme that illustrates a connection or interaction between them (e.g., "The kitty is playing with the yarn"). *Similarity* involved relating objects by citing similarity, either specific visual similarity (e.g., "These are both green," "These look alike," "These all have doors") or similarity more generally (e.g., "It's like this one," "These two go together," "These go together"). *Other* relations included contrast (pointing out how items differed in some way; e.g., "Now that's what kind of makes something a desk as opposed to a table"), counting two or more items (e.g., "One, two, three snakes"), or conjoining (relating objects by mentioning them in the same utterance, without tying them together in any further way; e.g., "There's a barn and a zebra"). However, conjoining two pictures by using the same name ("A cat and a cat") was coded as taxonomic, as was noncounting number use (e.g., "Two cars").

Each coding category could be used in combination with any other, with the exception of conjoining (which was used only if no other relations applied). For example, "These two [pointing to dolphins] are the same kind of an—, kind of beast, and this one [pointing to shark] is different, isn't it?" was coded as both taxonomic and contrasting; "The eels, they like water" was coded as both taxonomic and thematic. Agreement was calculated by having both coders code a randomly chosen subset of the transcripts. Agreement regarding the content of relations (including both mothers' and children's utterances) was 95% for Study 1 (based on 10 transcripts), 91% for Study 2 (based on 7 transcripts), and 98% for Study 3 (based on 14 transcripts).

### Content of Single-Object Statements

The content of single-object statements was coded as *ostension, thematic,* or *appearance.* Information is coded as *ostension* when an object is explicitly labeled or is referred to by its label (e.g., "This is a shark"). Information is coded as *thematic* when a single object is related to another object (either in the book or not pictured) or by speaking about a single object in a story-like fashion or as being involved in some activity or theme (e.g., "Your papa has one [wok] on the stove"). Information is coded as *appearance* when it refers to color, texture, substance, parts, shape, size, or any other visual property that was not captured in the relation coding (e.g., "A little, teeny, teeny ant").

When a statement about an individual object overlapped with a relation code, only the latter was coded. In other words, single-object codes were used only for those utterances that were not already coded as relations. Agreement regarding the content of single-object statements (including both mothers' and children's utterances) was 95% for Study 1 (based on eight transcripts), 95% for Study 2 (based on five transcripts), and 92% for Study 3 (based on five transcripts).

### Pictures Linked by Relations

This level of coding examined which of the four kinds of pictures in the custom-designed books of Studies 1 and 3 were related to one another (target$_1$, target$_2$, contrasting category, thematic associate). For example, "This is an anteater, and this is an anteater" relates the two within-target-category pictures; "That's a seal. It's like the walrus, OK?" relates a target-category picture to a contrasting-category picture. Coders made use of gestural information (e.g., pointing) to clarify ambiguous utterances (e.g., to determine the focus of deictics, such as *this* or *these*). We coded all relations between any two or more pictures. The custom-designed books were designed so that we could calculate the probabilities of producing each kind of relation, fully controlling for probability of occurrence assuming a random model. Thus, we could conduct statistical analyses to determine whether, for example, links among thematically related items were more common than links among contrasting-category items.

For the target category, we also used a separate picture code for statements referring to the category in general or an instance off the page (instead of one of the pictured instances), so as not to inflate the number of within-target-category relations. This distinction was not made for contrasting-category or thematic instances as, in these cases, it was less common for participants to refer to instances other than those pictured in the books.

### Pictures Referred to by Single-Object Statements

We also examined the focus of statements provided for pictures individually (e.g., "This is a shark"). Specifically, we coded whether statements about individual pictures concerned one of the target-category instances (e.g., *cat*), a contrasting-category instance (e.g., *raccoon*), or a thematic associate (e.g., *yarn*). As with content coding, single-object codes were used only for those utterances that were not already coded as relations. Agreement (for relations and individual pictures combined, for both mothers' and children's utterances) was 90% for Study 1 (based on 10 transcripts) and 92% for Study 3 (based on 14 transcripts).

### Types versus Tokens

Both relations and single-object statements were calculated as the number of types (not tokens) per page. So, instead of coding how many instances of each kind of relation occurred, we coded whether each kind of relation occurred at all (regardless of how often) on each page. For example, if a mother made two separate thematic relational statements linking the large cat and the yarn, she would be scored as producing one such (kind of) statement. The decision to code types rather than tokens was based primarily on two points. First, many relations were made across utterances rather than within a single utterance. Second, mothers sometimes repeated a statement fully or in part. Thus, we have provided a very conservative estimate of the number of such statements. Undoubtedly, mothers are providing more relational and single-object statements than are tallied with this method.

For the purposes of counting relation types, both picture codes and content codes were considered together. Thus, on the bat page, if a mother made two separate statements relating the two bats, once by referring to their basic-level taxonomic relatedness, and once by describing their perceptual similarity, these were coded as two separate relation types. However, if a mother made two separate statements relating the two bats, both referring to basic-level taxonomic relatedness, these counted as only *one* relation type. Similarly, a mother was counted as providing three separate relation types if she made three thematic statements, one relating $bat_1$ to the cave, another relating $bat_2$ to the cave, and a third relating both bats to the cave. Note that, for each page, there were potentially dozens of different relation types possible (multiplying the number of content codes by the number of combinations of picture codes).

## Presentation of Results

In the following analyses, all means represent types per 100 coded utterances unless otherwise noted. Also, all significant effects were followed up using Tukey HSD procedures unless otherwise noted.

## STUDY 1: CUSTOM-DESIGNED BOOKS WITH 35-MONTH-OLDS

### Content of Relations

In all, 526 maternal relations (tallying types, not tokens) were identified; taxonomic, thematic, and similarity relations accounted for 83% of them. We predicted that, if children are learning about category structure directly from mothers, then mothers should refer to taxonomic relations more frequently than other kinds of relations (thematic, similarity, contrasting, conjoining, counting). We further predicted that taxonomic relations would be more frequent for animal categories than for artifact categories.

A 2 (domain: animals, artifacts) × 3 (relation type: taxonomic [including all three levels], thematic, similarity) ANOVA was conducted. The dependent measure was the number of relations produced divided by the total number of coded utterances for that speaker and domain (e.g., for participant X, we divided the total number of taxonomic, thematic, and similarity relations that X produced by the total number of coded utterances that X produced for the animal domain). This correction controls for domain differences in the frequency of speech overall (as can be seen in Table 5 above). There were significant effects for domain ($F[1, 15] = 18.06$, $p < .001$), relation type ($F[2, 30] = 36.58$, $p < .0001$), and domain × relation type ($F[2, 30] = 7.41$, $p <$

39

.005; see Figure 2a). Overall, taxonomic relations and thematic relations were much more frequent than similarity relations. Thus, taxonomic relations were frequent but were not privileged. As predicted, taxonomic relations were more common for animals than for artifacts ($p < .01$). Unexpectedly, thematic relations were also more common for animals than for artifacts ($p < .01$). However, the similarity relations do not differ between animals and artifacts.

### Role of Similarity in Patterns of Relations

Pretesting of the book pages showed that same-category animal pictures (e.g., two horses) were more similar overall than same-category artifact pictures (e.g., two desks; see the Appendix). Therefore, we performed an analysis using just those animal and artifact items that had overlapping within-category similarity scores (within the range of 3.8–5.9). There were seven such items for animals (cat, horse, crab, seal, anteater, eel, and dolphin; within-category similarity scores ranging from 3.92 to 5.50; $M = 4.72$) and four items for artifacts (sneaker, wok, safe, and tongs; within-category similarity scores ranging from 3.83 to 5.83; $M = 4.81$). (Another advantage of this analysis is that it includes only pictures with single-word labels. That is, although some of the artifact pictures in the full set are labeled with compound nouns [e.g., *boot-car*], such items are excluded in this analysis, thereby rendering the two domains more comparable.) On the remaining seven items (two animals, five artifacts), scores did not overlap: the within-category similarity scores for animals were higher than the within-category similarity scores for *any* of the artifacts (i.e., all were higher than 5.90), and the within-category similarity scores for artifacts were lower than the within-category similarity scores for *any* of the animals (i.e., all were lower than 3.80).

We conducted a paired $t$ test, considering just the subset of items for which animal and artifact similarity scores overlapped and for which the mean within-category similarity scores for animals and artifacts were equal. Again, we controlled for the number of coded utterances produced in each domain. On this comparison, taxonomic relations were still more frequent for animals than for artifacts ($M$'s = 9.54 and 5.96, respectively, $t$ paired [15] = 2.73, $p < .02$). Thus, the domain difference cannot be attributed to greater similarity among the animal pictures.

### Taxonomic Level

Most of the taxonomic relations produced by mothers were basic level. Specifically, of 201 taxonomic relations produced by mothers, 163 were basic level, 31 were superordinate level, and 7 were subordinate level. Most of the

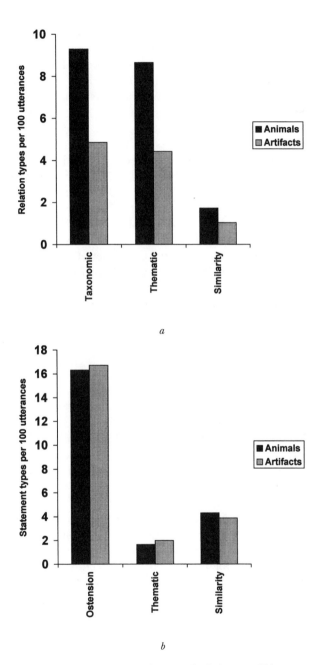

FIGURE 2.—*a*, Study 1, mean number of maternal relations per 100 utterances, as a function of content and domain. *b*, Study 1, mean number of maternal statement types about individual pictures, per 100 utterances, as a function of content and domain.

maternal nonbasic relations referred to animals (31 of 38). Therefore, it is possible that the domain differences found above were due to the greater number of nonbasic taxonomic relations for the animal domain. To examine this possibility, we reanalyzed the taxonomic relations, this time excluding all nonbasic taxonomic relations. We conducted a paired $t$ test comparing animal basic-level taxonomic relations with artifact basic-level taxonomic relations, again correcting for the amount of speech per domain by dividing by the total number of coded utterances for that speaker and domain. Importantly, basic-level taxonomic relations were significantly more frequent for animals than for artifacts ($M$'s = 7.34 and 4.37, respectively, $t$ paired [15] = 3.61, $p < .005$). Thus, the domain differences found earlier cannot be attributed to nonbasic levels.

We also conducted an additional analysis on the basic-level taxonomic relations, as a control for within-target-category similarity, as before. We conducted a paired $t$ test, considering just the subset of items for which animal and artifact similarity scores overlapped (see above), again controlling for the number of coded utterances produced in each domain. On this comparison, basic-level taxonomic relations were still more frequent for animals than for artifacts ($M$'s = 7.49 and 5.34, respectively, $t$ paired [15] = 2.08, $p = .0275$, one tailed).

### Content of Statements about Individuals

It is important to show that patterns of results for relations do not simply mirror patterns of statements about individual pictures. To address this issue, we conducted a 2 (domain: animal, artifact) × 3 (statement type: ostension, thematic, appearance) ANOVA on maternal statements about individual pictures. Once again, scores were adjusted to control for the amount of speech per domain (by dividing by the total number of coded utterances in each domain). There was a main effect for statement type only ($F[2, 30] = 101.64$, $p < .0001$; see Figure 2$b$). Ostension was more common than either thematic or appearance statements ($p < .01$). Importantly, there were no effects of domain. Thus, patterns for relations between pictures differ from, and do not simply mirror, patterns for speech about individual pictures.

### Pictures Linked by Relations

We turn now to examining which pictures were linked by relations. Maternal relations included three kinds: relations between two pictures ($N = 283$); relations between multiple pictures, including both target-category instances ($N = 133$); and other relations ($N = 110$). In this section, only the first two kinds of relations will be analyzed further.[4]

### Relations between Two Pictures

Our main prediction here is that, if maternal input stresses the importance of richly structured taxonomic categories, relations between the two target-category pictures should be more common than any other relations linking two pictures. Furthermore, if input highlights domain differences, mothers should relate the two target-category pictures more often for animal than for artifact items.

When we consider just those relations linking two pictures (e.g., those linking the two target-category pictures [e.g., two horses] or those linking a target-category picture with a contrasting-category picture [e.g., horse and zebra]), the theoretical probability of participants relating two target-category pictures (e.g., two horses) is one in six; the theoretical probability of relating a target-category picture to a contrasting-category picture (e.g., a horse and a zebra) is two in six; and the theoretical probability of relating a target-category picture with a thematic-associate picture (e.g., a horse and a barn) is also two in six. There is also theoretically a one in six probability of relating the contrasting-category picture with the thematic-associate picture (e.g., a zebra and a barn), although there is no intended link between those pictures.

In order to control for the a priori probabilities noted above, we calculated four scores for each participant, separately for animals and artifacts: (*a*) the total number of relation types between the two target-category pictures (henceforth *within-target-category relations*); (*b*) the sum of all relation types between a target-category picture and the thematic-associate picture divided by two (henceforth *target-plus-thematic-associate relations*); (*c*) the sum of all relation types between a target-category picture and the contrasting-

---

[4] The remaining relations included (*a*) those linking one of the target-category pictures to the contrasting-category and thematic-associate pictures, but excluding the other target-category picture (e.g., a relation linking a horse, a zebra, and a barn), and (*b*) all cases in which the target category (e.g., horses) was mentioned but did not refer clearly to either of the instances pictured on the page. These were excluded from further consideration for several reasons: A separate statistical analysis of these relations yielded no interpretable patterns (e.g., no particular relation type, domain, or level of familiarity predominated). Furthermore, when these relations were combined with the relations linking two pictures (e.g., adding relations about horses [without referring to those on the page] to relations linking the two horses depicted on the page), it did not change the patterns or findings from the two-place relations. Finally, these remaining relations were infrequent (for mothers, the mean number of relations per domain, relation type, and familiarity level never reached 0.8, as compared to means of 3.5 and more for relations linking two pictures). Given that we had no predictions or theoretical context for interpreting results of these relations, they were not considered further.

category picture divided by two (henceforth *target-plus-contrasting-category relations*); and (*d*) the total number of relation types between a thematic-associate picture and a contrasting-category picture (henceforth *thematic-plus-contrasting relations*). Thus, with the adjustments described above, the a priori probability of producing each of the four scores is roughly equal.[5] As with the content analyses, we divided each of these four scores by the total number of coded utterances for that speaker and domain in order to control for amount of speech in each domain.

These scores were entered into an ANOVA containing two factors: domain (animals, artifacts) and relation type (within category, target plus thematic associate, target plus contrasting category, and thematic plus contrasting). There were main effects for domain ($F[1, 15] = 8.98$, $p < .01$) and for relation type ($F[3, 45] = 97.20$, $p < .0001$) and a domain $\times$ relation type interaction ($F[3, 45] = 18.90$, $p < .0001$). As predicted, within-category relations were more common than all other relations, for both animals and artifacts separately ($p < .01$). Also as predicted, within-category relations were more common for the animals than for the artifacts ($p < .01$) (see Figure 3).

### Role of Similarity in Patterns of Relations between Two Pictures

We conducted a paired *t* test, considering just the subset of items for which animal and artifact similarity scores overlapped and for which the mean within-category similarity scores for animals and artifacts were equal. Again, we controlled for the number of coded utterances produced in each domain. On this comparison, although there was a tendency for mothers to produce more within-target-category relation types for animals ($M = 9.65$) than for artifacts ($M = 7.76$), this difference was not significant. However, a closer inspection of the data suggested that the contrasting relations were responsible for the null effect. Recall that contrasting relations are those for which the speaker explicitly mentions how the two instances *differ* from one another and thus are not predicted to be higher for animals than for artifacts. When reanalyzing the data without the contrasting relations, we find a significant domain difference in the predicted direction, with more within-

[5] The probability is not exactly equal because relations involving the contrasting-category picture and/or the thematic-associate picture could include general reference to the entire contrasting or thematic category (e.g., birds in general or caves in general) as well as specific reference to the objects pictured in the books. In contrast, for the target category, relations were restricted specifically to those referring to the objects pictured in the books. Thus, there is a somewhat lesser a priori probability of producing within-target-category relations than the other three. However, within-target-category relations were produced more frequently despite the slight bias against such a finding.

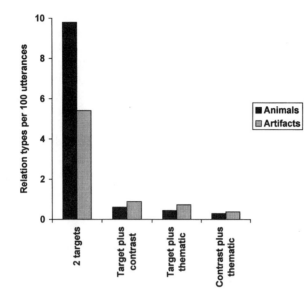

FIGURE 3.—Study 1, mean number of maternal relation types involving two pictures per 100 coded utterances, as a function of domain and relation type. (Scores were adjusted to account for the a priori probability of producing each type.)

target-category relation types for animals than for artifacts ($M$'s = 8.61 and 6.46, respectively, $t[15]$ = 2.19, $p < .05$). We conclude, therefore, that the domain differences in number of within-category relation types reported earlier were not simply the result of domain differences in within-category similarity. Domain differences persist even when the domains are equated for within-category similarity.

### Relations among Multiple Pictures

We also analyzed those relations linking both target-category pictures with either or both of the remaining pictures (e.g., horses plus zebra, horses plus barn, and horses plus zebra plus barn). The scope of these relations is potentially taxonomic (because they include two instances of the same category), yet they are more inclusive than the relations linking two pictures, analyzed above. Thus, we predicted that they could occur more often with animals than with artifacts. The number of each type of relation, corrected for number of coded utterances per domain, was entered into a 2 (domain: animal, artifact) × 3 (relation type: targets plus contrasting picture, targets plus thematic picture, all pictures) ANOVA. Significant effects were obtained for both factors and the interaction ($p$'s < .005). More relation types were used for animals ($M = 2.24$) than for artifacts ($M = 0.66$), as predicted, although significant domain differences were obtained only for targets-plus-contrasting-picture and targets-plus-thematic-picture relations (both $p$'s < .005, simple-effects test). Targets-plus-contrasting-picture relation types ($M = 2.69$) were more common than either targets-plus-thematic-picture ($M = 0.72$) or all-picture ($M = 0.93$) relation types ($p$'s < .01). These results suggest that, as predicted, mothers place greater emphasis on animals than on artifacts with respect to taxonomic groupings that include basic-level categories as a subset.

### Statements about Individual Pictures

Mothers might dwell on relations between the target-category pictures simply because those pictures are the most salient rather than because of any systematic preference for taxonomic categories per se. If so, we would expect to find more speech *in general* about the target-category pictures than about the contrasting or thematic pictures. To test this, we conducted a 2 (domain: animal, artifact) × 3 (picture type: target-category picture, contrasting-category picture, thematic-associate picture) ANOVA. As with the earlier analyses, the scores were adjusted to make responses to each of the picture types equivalent. Specifically, statements about the two target-category pictures were summed, then divided by two; statements about the contrasting-category and the thematic-associate pictures were simply summed. Also as before, the scores were adjusted to control for the number of coded utterances in each domain. The analysis yielded a main effect for picture type only ($F[2, 30] = 13.30$, $p < .0001$), indicating that there were fewer statements about single objects for the target-category picture ($M = 8.75$) than for either the contrasting-category picture ($M = 15.10$) or the thematic-associate picture ($M = 12.73$, both $p$'s < .01), but the latter two did not differ significantly from one another. Thus, preference for within-target-category relations was not due to salience of target-category pictures. Likewise, domain differences in relations regarding the target-category instances were specific to relations rather than to the individual pictures included in the relations.

### Correspondences between Content of Relations and Pictures Linked by Relations

To this point, our analyses examined the content of relations separately from the pictures referred to. Here, we integrate the two levels of analysis, obtaining information that cannot be derived from either of the analyses considered separately. The combined analyses allow us to address such issues as what *kind* of information mothers provide when they talk about instances from the same category as well as *which pictures* mothers group together when they provide taxonomic or thematic information. In principle, it is possible to examine all the data in this light (every content category crossed with every picture combination, in a large grid). However, this would be neither useful nor manageable given the large number of cells and especially the large number of empty cells. Therefore, we approached the question more selectively, from two different directions. It should be noted that the two types of analyses presented below examine the same data set from overlapping vantage points.

The first approach is to examine the content of within-target-category relations (relations linking the two same-category instances, e.g., two horses). Within-target-category relations are of special interest because they link items that belong to the same taxonomic category. The question, then, is what information mothers provide when linking these items. Do mothers typically provide taxonomic information, as predicted? The second approach is to examine which pictures are linked for each of the two most common kinds of relations: taxonomic and thematic. In other words, when mothers talk about taxonomic or about thematic links, which groupings of items are selected?

### Content of within-Target-Category Relations

If mothers emphasize taxonomic categories, most within-target-category relations should be taxonomic in content. To find out whether they are, we conducted a 2 (domain: animals, artifacts) $\times$ 4 (content: taxonomic, thematic, similarity, contrast) ANOVA on the number of relations linking within-target-category pictures, controlling for the number of coded utterances in each domain. Both factors are within subject. We obtained significant effects for domain ($F[1, 15] = 16.74$, $p < .001$), content ($F[3, 45] = 63.62$, $p < .0001$), and domain $\times$ content ($F[3, 45] = 14.71$, $p < .0001$). Below, we discuss just those effects involving content because the domain effects were previously considered in the section examining relations analyzed by picture type.

As predicted, relations linking within-target-category pictures more frequently mentioned taxonomic information ($M = 5.55$) than thematic ($M = 0.74$), similarity ($M = 0.27$), or contrast ($M = 0.95$) information ($p < .01$); the latter three kinds of relations did not differ from one another. In other words, when talking about how the two same-category pictures relate, mothers primarily mentioned taxonomic relatedness. Also as predicted, when linking within-target-category pictures, mothers provided more taxonomic relation types for animals than for artifacts ($M$'s = 7.30 and 3.82, respectively, $p < .01$). There were no domain differences for thematic, similarity, or contrast relations.

*Taxonomic and Thematic Relations Analyzed by Picture Type*

The data are presented in Figure 4. The majority of taxonomic relations were provided for within-target-category pictures, whereas thematic relations were spread much more evenly across picture types (although more often for target-plus-thematic pictures than for any other picture combinations). Interestingly, mothers commonly invoked thematic relations for picture combinations that did not include the thematic-associate picture at all (41% of animal thematic and 26% of artifact thematic relations were for such picture combinations).[6] Moreover, a sizable proportion of mothers' thematic relations (43% for animals and 21% for artifacts) referred to picture combinations that included *both* target-category pictures, suggesting that thematic relations may often *presuppose* taxonomic groupings rather than being in conflict with them.

We next report statistical analyses comparing taxonomic and thematic relations directly. As predicted, taxonomic relations were more likely than thematic relations to involve linking the two target-category pictures to one another (e.g., the two bats). Specifically, 79% of mothers' taxonomic relations but only 10% of their thematic relations were of this sort ($F[1, 15] = 120.06$, $p < .0001$). There were no significant effects involving domain. Also as predicted, thematic relations were more likely than taxonomic relations to involve linking the target category (either one of the target-category pictures or the target category without reference to a picture) to the thematic associate (e.g., a bat with the cave). Specifically, 43% of mothers' thematic relations and none of their taxonomic relations were of this sort ($p < .001$, binomial test). Moreover, examining just the thematic relations alone, we find that relations of this sort (linking target category to thematic associate) were more frequent for artifacts (55% of thematic relations) than for animals (32% of thematic relations, $t[15] = 3.60$, $p < .005$). To put this another way, thematic relations focusing strictly on the thematic association were more common for artifacts than for animals.

Finally, we examined how often mothers formed a relation that *included* (as a subset) the two target-category pictures[7]—for example, both bats plus

---

[6] These relations include all those referred to as "two targets" plus a subset of the relations referred to as "two targets plus other" and "all other." Because only some of the "two targets plus other" and "all other" relations exclude the thematic-associate pictures, the numbers provided here cannot be derived from the figures.

[7] For the purposes of these analyses, we exclude those relations referring to nonpictured instances of the target category. Many of these involved reference to the category as a whole (e.g., "Bats live in caves") and so would be appropriate. However, this coding category also included specific instances that are not depicted (e.g., "Remember we saw a bat like that in a cave"), so, to be conservative, we have excluded the entire coding category. Had we included these relations, however, it would have made the argument even stronger, as these were particularly frequent for animals.

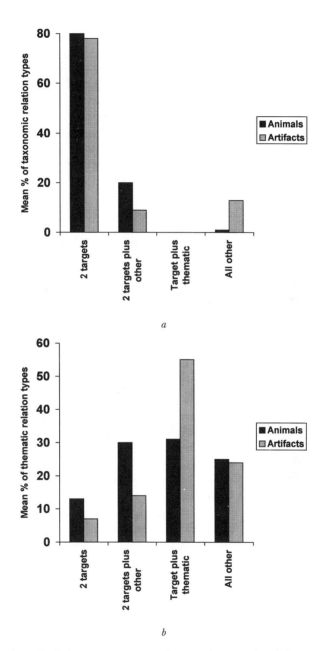

FIGURE 4.—*a,* Study 1, mean percentage of maternal taxonomic relation types as a function of domain and picture type. *b,* Study 1, mean percentage of maternal thematic relation types as a function of domain and picture type.

the bird, both bats plus the cave, or all four pictures. These relations are of theoretical interest because they incorporate the taxonomic category and may even build on it. Thematic relations were more likely than taxonomic relations to refer to this configuration of pictures ($M$'s = 22% and 14%, respectively, $F[1, 15] = 7.33, p < .02$). Furthermore, such relations were proportionately more frequent for animals than for artifacts ($M$'s = 25% and 12%, respectively, $F[1, 15] = 16.96, p < .001$). This last result suggests that, even when producing thematic relations, mothers focused (implicitly) on taxonomic categories more frequently for animals than for artifacts. There was no significant interaction between domain and content.

## Children's Questions and Relations

Although our primary focus is maternal input, children's data also provide relevant supplementary information concerning who is leading the topic of conversations (mothers or children). Children's data also are informative regarding mother-child mismatches, thus indirectly suggesting areas in which children's biases differ from those of their mothers.

Specifically, we examined two primary issues. The first issue is whether maternal emphasis on taxonomic relations is spontaneous or is instead elicited by children's questions. To address this issue, we examined how often children's questions focused on one instance as opposed to plural instances and how often they focused on taxonomic category membership, thematic relatedness, and appearances or similarity. If children's questions are responsible for the structure of maternal input, then children should often be requesting information about plural instances, not just single instances, and they should be asking equally often about taxonomic categories and thematic relatedness (rarely appearances or similarity).

The second major issue is whether there are convergences or mismatches between mothers' and children's speech. If mothers' data show patterns not present in the children's data, this suggests areas in which maternal input may have an effect. If children's data show patterns not present in maternal input, this suggests areas in which children exhibit biases that do not result from explicit guidance. If mothers' and children's data show similar patterns, further research will be needed to determine whether this reflects a mutual bias or learning that has already occurred. To examine convergences and mismatches, we compared mothers and children with respect to both content of relational statements and pictures linked by relational statements.

### Children's Questions

In order to assess the degree to which children elicit taxonomic information, we coded all children's on-task questions ($M = 13.06$ for the animal book, $M = 7.75$ for the artifact book). Questions that simply repeated part of an immediately preceding question posed by the mother (e.g., "What?" in response to the mother's "What's that called?") were not coded further; these accounted for 8% of the questions about the animal book and 10% of the questions about the artifact book. The remaining questions were coded along two dimensions: whether they referred to a single individual, more than one individual, or other; and whether the content was taxonomic (concerning either identity [e.g., "What's this?"] or category information), thematic, appearance based, or other. Coding agreement was calculated taking into account the results of the work of a second coder, who coded three of the transcripts. Agreement regarding number of referents (single, plural, or other) was 85%; agreement regarding content of questions was 93%.

If maternal relations were elicited by the children, then children's questions should have focused frequently on taxonomic and thematic information regarding multiple instances. In fact, this was not the case. The majority of questions were taxonomic and concerned a single object or individual (66% for the animal book, 65% for the artifact book). A 2 (domain) $\times$ 3 (referent: individual, plural, other) $\times$ 4 (content: taxonomic, thematic, similarity, other) within-subject ANOVA was conducted on children's questions, controlling for the number of coded utterances each child produced per domain. The ANOVA revealed significant effects for each factor except domain and for all interactions, including those involving domain (all $p$'s $< .05$). Questions about the taxonomic status of individuals occurred more frequently than all other types of questions and more frequently for animals than for artifacts. Questions about a single individual greatly outnumbered questions about more than one individual ($M$'s $= 15.53$ and $3.57$, respectively, for animals and $10.59$ and $2.27$, respectively, for artifacts). Furthermore, means of $15.14$ questions about animals and $10.49$ questions about artifacts were taxonomic, $1.43$ and $1.56$, respectively, were thematic, and $0.21$ and $0$, respectively, concerned similarity. Thus, children's questions focused on the names for individual items. We conclude that maternal focus on taxonomic and thematic relations was rarely elicited directly by the child.

## Content of Relations: Mothers and Children

Focusing on just the relational statements, we performed a 2 (speaker: mother, child) $\times$ 2 (domain: animal, artifact) $\times$ 3 (content: taxonomic, thematic, similarity) ANOVA to examine the possibility of mother-child differences in domain effects and/or content focus. (Note that this analysis is confined to taxonomic, thematic, or similarity relations as there are too few instances of other relations to analyze further.) As before, all scores were corrected for the amount of speech produced by dividing by the number of

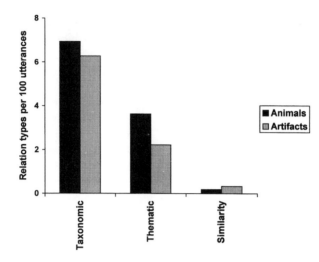

FIGURE 5.—Study 1, mean number of children's relation types per 100 coded utterances, as a function of domain and content.

coded utterances produced by each speaker per domain. For results, see Figure 2*a* above and Figure 5. We report just those effects that involve speaker.

As expected, mothers produced significantly more relation types than children ($M$'s = 15.00 and 9.80, respectively, $F[1, 15] = 13.07$, $p < .005$). More important was a significant speaker × domain interaction ($F[1, 15] = 6.48$, $p < .05$). In contrast to the mothers, who provided more relation types for animals than for artifacts ($p < .001$, simple-effects test), children showed no significant domain difference ($p > .20$). Finally, there was also a speaker × content interaction ($F[2, 30] = 4.37$, $p < .05$). Whereas for mothers taxonomic and thematic relations occurred equally often (N.S.), for children taxonomic relations were more frequent than thematic relations ($p < .01$). Moreover, thematic relations were produced more frequently by mothers than by children ($p < .01$), whereas there were no significant mother-child differences in the frequency of taxonomic or similarity relations.

### Children's Relations: Solo versus Scaffolded

Children's relations, characterized above, included two kinds. First are those that were constructed by the child (*solo* relations)—for example,

Child: Here's, here's some squirrels [pointing to both squirrels].

Second are those for which the mothers provided an initial frame (*scaffolded* relations)—for example,

52

Mother: Who puts the ball on their nose? Do you remember?
Child: A seal.

Mother: How many squirrels are there?
Child: One, two, three [pointing to both squirrels and the chipmunk].

Both solo and scaffolded relations were credited to the child because children completed the relations by providing the relevant information. However, because the two types of relations differ in the extent to which mothers and children framed the content of the relation, we examined whether solo and scaffolded relations differed in content.

To address this question, we determined, for each child and each relation type (taxonomic, thematic, or other), the percentage of relations of each type that were solo and scaffolded, then calculated the mean for that relation type (excluding from consideration those children who produced no relations of that type). Thus, of the 16 children who produced at least one taxonomic relation, 95% of the taxonomic relations produced were solo. In contrast, of the 13 children who produced at least one thematic relation, only 55% of the thematic relations produced were solo. Of the 11 children who produced at least one other (nontaxonomic, nonthematic) relation, 77% of these other relations were solo. The difference between thematic and taxonomic relations was significant ($t$ paired [12] = 4.14, $p < .005$). These results imply that thematic relations were less frequently produced *spontaneously* by children and often emerged as the result of maternal scaffolding.

### Pictures Linked by Taxonomic Relations: Mothers and Children

An important aspect of the books was that each page was designed to include appearance-reality mismatches that would encourage mothers to talk about deeper, nonobvious features (e.g., a bird was included on the bat page because birds and bats are similar in appearance but members of distinct categories). We hypothesized, therefore, that children would make many categorization errors (e.g., referring to both a bird and a bat as *birds*). This can be examined by tallying how often children's (as opposed to mothers') taxonomic relations linked either (*a*) one target picture with another (e.g., two bats), which is appropriate for a basic-level relation, or (*b*) one or both target pictures with a contrasting-category instance (e.g., a bat and a bird or both bats and a bird), which is inappropriate for a basic-level relation. (Although links of type *b* are appropriate for superordinate-level categories, children produced very few superordinate-level taxonomic relations and proportionately fewer than mothers.)

As predicted, children were much less likely than mothers to link both target pictures in their taxonomic relations (for animals: $M$'s = 35% and 80%, respectively, $t$ paired [15] = 4.78, $p < .0005$; for artifacts: $M$'s = 27% and 78%, respectively, $t$ paired [15] = 5.07, $p < .0005$). Also as predicted, children were much more likely than mothers to link one or both target pictures with a contrasting-category instance in their taxonomic relations (for animals: $M$'s = 57% and 20%, respectively, $t$ paired [15] = 3.26, $p < .01$; for artifacts: $M$'s = 64% and 27%, respectively, $t$ paired [15] = 4.17, $p < .001$). Thus, as anticipated, children often erred in determining the appropriate category boundaries for these picture sets.

## Summary: Study 1 Relations

All mothers made statements explicitly relating two or more entities (mean of 33 relation types per mother, or 16.5 per book). When focusing on the type of information provided, we found that taxonomic and thematic relations were equivalent in frequency. In contrast, when focusing on which pictures were linked, we found a powerful preference to link same-category instances (two bats) rather than a picture with its thematic associate (bat and cave). The overwhelming majority of the time, when mothers formed relations linking two pictures, they chose to link same-category instances.

Although these two sets of results may seem contradictory, they can be explained by examining Figure 4 above. As expected, mothers tended to focus (nearly 80% of the time) on the two same-category instances when providing taxonomic information. In contrast, mothers talked about thematic relations for a wide array of different picture combinations, only about half of which included the canonical case of a picture and its thematic associate. Thus, relations linking a picture and its thematic associate were relatively rare, but thematic relations emerged for a range of other contexts.

Thus, as predicted, when mothers linked two pictures, they tended to link those that were taxonomically related. However, contrary to our initial predictions, there was no evidence that mothers stressed taxonomic over thematic groupings in their talk. (Indeed, mothers were even more likely to focus on thematic groupings than were children; see the discussion of mother-child mismatches below.) In part, the equal frequency of thematic and taxonomic statements may be the result of the fact that thematic statements often included reference to taxonomic groupings, meaning that thematic and taxonomic groupings are not wholly distinct. For example, mothers might say, *Bats live in caves*, which conveys a thematic relation between a *taxonomic category* and a thematic associate. Further support for the idea that thematic links often build on taxonomic ones is that many of mothers' thematic relations (over a third) were produced for picture combinations that included *both* target-category pictures. This suggests that, rather than necessarily being in conflict with taxonomic relations, thematic relations can serve to describe and enhance them.

## Domain Differences

As predicted, there were striking domain differences in maternal relations. When examining relation *content,* both taxonomic and thematic relations were more common for animals than for artifacts. The domain difference is robust, holding up when controlling for amount of talk about each domain, within-category similarity in each domain, and taxonomic level of categories in each domain. Similarly, when examining *pictures* linked by relations, mothers were also more likely to relate same-category instances for animals than for artifacts (even when discussing thematic relations). Thus, mothers were more likely to emphasize the taxonomic relatedness of two animals than of two artifacts. Again, this result held up when controlling for the amount of talk in each domain, within-category similarity, and level of taxonomic relations (i.e., examining basic-level taxonomic relations). Finally, the domain differences cannot be explained in terms of the attention paid to each picture individually as maternal input about individual objects revealed no domain differences whatsoever.

## Mother-Child Mismatches

An examination of children's relations revealed three primary mother-child differences. First, as predicted, children made more naming errors than mothers (as can be seen by how often their taxonomic relations included same-category instances). Second, unlike the mothers, children did not consistently distinguish between animals and artifacts when focusing on taxonomic categories. Although past work has shown that children clearly understand animate-inanimate distinctions by age 3 and even earlier (see Gelman, 1990; Golinkoff, Harding, Carlson, & Sexton, 1984), such differences did not emerge in children's relational statements in this context.

Third, and in contrast to claims of a thematic-to-taxonomic shift, children were actually less likely than mothers to focus on thematic relations, in both a relative and an absolute sense. Indeed, children were more likely to focus on taxonomic than thematic relations, whereas mothers focused on the two kinds of relations equally. Mothers produced more thematic relations than children, when controlling for the amount of talk of each speaker, but did not produce more taxonomic or similarity relations. When children did produce thematic relations, they were often the result of maternal scaffolding (rather than having been produced independently). Nor were thematic statements elicited by children's questions, which focused primarily on names for individual objects.

We turn next to maternal relations in Study 2, which provides a replication using commercially available picture books.

## STUDY 2: COMMERCIAL BOOKS WITH 35-MONTH-OLDS

It is unclear how accurately the books used in Study 1 represent the input that mothers ordinarily provide while reading picture books together with their small children. Specifically, by clearly presenting two members of one category alongside another member of a similar but contrasting category, we may have biased participants to dwell on taxonomic relations. Study 2, using commercially prepared picture books, allowed us to address this question. If the same patterns of results emerge in Study 2 as in Study 1, it suggests that the findings are general and not simply an artifact of the custom-designed stimuli.

For Study 2, we did not code by picture (i.e., target-category pictures vs. contrasting-category picture vs. thematic-associate picture) given that the pages of these books were not structured to allow for such analyses. Also, coding was restricted to those utterances referring to items that were the focus of the book (i.e., animals in *Farm Animals;* vehicles in *The Truck Book*) and the subject of the sentence in question. We did this because the books had many incidental pictures (e.g., people buying ice cream from the ice-cream truck) and we wished to maintain a clear comparison between the two domains. Otherwise, coding was identical to that of Study 1.

### Content of Relations between Pictures

In all, 397 maternal relations (tallying types, not tokens) were identified; taxonomic, thematic, and similarity relations accounted for 90% of them. As before, we predicted that mothers would produce many taxonomic relations, particularly for the farm animal book.

A 2 (domain: farm animals, trucks) $\times$ 3 (relation type: taxonomic, thematic, similarity) ANOVA was conducted. The dependent measure was the number of relation types divided by the total number of coded utterances per speaker and domain. We predicted that taxonomic relations would be discussed more frequently than thematic or similarity relations, especially for farm animals. There were significant effects for relation type ($F[2, 26] = 50.21$, $p < .0001$), domain ($F[1, 13] = 13.36$, $p < .005$), and domain $\times$ relation type ($F[2, 26] = 8.05$, $p < .005$; see Figure 6a). Similarity relations were less frequent than either taxonomic or thematic relations ($p < .01$), whereas the latter two did not differ from one another. Moreover, taxonomic relations were more common for the farm animal book than for the truck book ($p < .01$). None of the other domain comparisons were significant. In short, as in Study 1, and in line with our predictions, mothers stressed taxonomic and thematic relations over similarity relations. Furthermore, they stressed taxonomic relations more for animals than for artifacts.

### Taxonomic Level

Most of the taxonomic relations produced by mothers were basic level (66% for farm animals, 70% for trucks). Specifically, of 162 taxonomic relations produced by mothers, 110 were basic level, 51 were subordinate level, and only 1 was superordinate level. Most of the nonbasic relations (65%) were found when reading the farm animal book. The majority of these designated kinship relations or age-based groupings (e.g., *baby pigs, mommy goats, ducklings*). Therefore, it is possible that the domain differences found above were due to the greater number of nonbasic taxonomic relations for the animal domain. To examine this possibility, we conducted a paired $t$ test comparing basic-level taxonomic relations in the farm animal book with basic-level taxonomic relations in the truck book, again correcting for the amount of talk per domain by dividing by the total number of coded utterances for that speaker and domain. On this comparison, basic-level taxonomic relations were significantly more frequent for animals than for artifacts ($M$'s = 6.80 and 3.42, respectively, $t$ paired [13] = 2.49, $p < .05$). Thus, domain differences in taxonomic relations persist when holding taxonomic level constant.

### Statements Regarding Individuals

As was discussed in Study 1, in order to clarify the results for relational statements, it is important to show that the pattern of results for relations is not simply a reflection of individual item naming. In order to confirm this, a 2 (domain: farm animals, trucks) × 3 (code: ostension, thematic, appearance) ANOVA was conducted. Results are shown in Figure 6b. The dependent measure was the number of single-object statements divided by the number of coded utterances per participant and domain. There were significant effects of domain ($F[1, 13] = 19.36$, $p < .001$), code type ($F[2, 26] = 26.08$, $p < .0001$), and domain × code type ($F[2, 26] = 21.58$, $p < .0001$). Ostensive statements were more frequent than appearance or thematic statements, although this was especially true for trucks. The only significant domain difference was for ostension, with more ostension about trucks than about farm

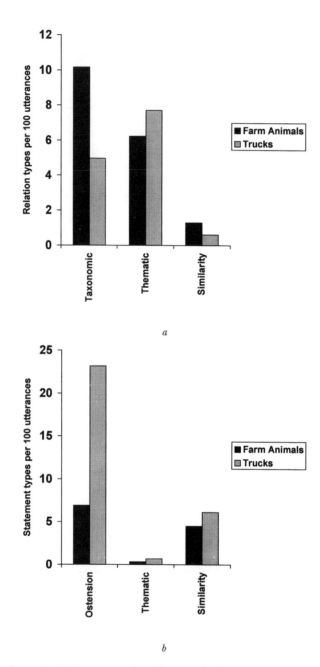

FIGURE 6.—*a,* Study 2, mean number of maternal relation types per 100 coded utterances, as a function of domain and content. *b,* Study 2, mean number of maternal statement types about individual pictures per 100 utterances, as a function of content and domain.

animals ($p < .001$, simple-effects test). Strikingly, the domain effect for ostension is in the opposite direction as the domain effect for taxonomic relations. Thus, the relational results do not merely reflect a pattern of individual item naming. Most important, domain differences in relations were specific to relations rather than to the individual pictures included in the relations.

### Children's Questions and Relations

As in Study 1, children's data were examined to discover what information children were eliciting and to probe for mother-child mismatches. First, we examined the content and nature of children's questions to determine whether maternal emphasis on taxonomic relations is spontaneous or is instead elicited by the children. The second major question is whether there are convergences or mismatches in mothers' and children's speech.

### Children's Questions

As in Study 1, we coded all children's on-task questions ($M$'s = 8.36 for the animal book and 11.86 for the artifact book). As before, questions that simply repeated part of an immediately preceding question posed by the mother were not coded further; these accounted for 6% of the questions that arose while reading the animal book and 7% of the questions that arose while reading the artifact book. The remaining questions were again coded along two dimensions: whether they referred to a single individual, more than one individual, or other and whether the content was taxonomic, thematic, appearance, or other. Coding agreement was calculated between the primary coder and a second coder, who coded three of the transcripts. Agreement regarding number of referents (single, plural, or other) was 100%; agreement regarding content of questions was also 100%.

As with Study 1, if maternal relations were elicited by the children, then children's questions should have focused frequently on taxonomic and thematic information regarding multiple instances. Again, this was not the case. A 2 (domain) × 3 (referent: individual, plural, other) × 4 (content: taxonomic, thematic, similarity, other) within-subjects ANOVA was conducted, controlling for amount of speech by dividing by the number of child-coded utterances per speaker and domain. This analysis revealed significant main effects for referent and content and significant referent × content and referent × domain interactions. The main effect of referent revealed that questions regarding single individuals were more numerous than both other kinds ($M$'s = 27.07 questions per 100 coded utterances for single individuals, 8.67 for plurals, and 4.28 for others). The main effect of content was due to the predominance of taxonomic over thematic, similarity, or other kinds of questions ($M$'s = 25.26, 2.74, 1.50, and 10.52, respectively). The interaction showed that taxonomic questions regarding individuals were more numerous than all other kinds ($M$'s = 25.86 for taxonomic questions as opposed to a mean of 0.89 for all others). There was also a domain × reference interaction, revealing that taxonomic questions regarding individuals were more frequent for artifacts than for animals. To sum up, despite domain variations, the most frequent kind of question concerned the names for individual items. Thus, maternal focus on taxonomic and thematic relations was rarely elicited directly by the child.

### Content of Relations: Mothers and Children

For these analyses, we examine only those effects involving speaker. We conducted a 2 (speaker: mother, child) × 2 (domain: animal, artifact) × 3 (content: taxonomic, thematic, similarity) ANOVA. There were no significant effects involving speaker.

### Children's Relations: Solo versus Scaffolded

As in Study 1, children's relations were coded as either *solo* (constructed by the child) or *scaffolded* (initially framed by the mother). We again examined whether solo and scaffolded relations differ in content. For each child and each relation type (taxonomic, thematic, or other), we calculated the percentage of relations of each type that were solo (as opposed to scaffolded), then calculated the mean for that relation type (excluding from consideration those children who produced no relations of that type). Thus, of the 12 children who produced at least one taxonomic relation, 96% of the taxonomic relations produced were solo. In contrast, of the 13 children who produced at least one thematic relation, only 55% of the thematic relations produced were solo. The difference between thematic and taxonomic relations was significant ($t$ paired [12] = 5.18, $p < .001$). Of the eight children who produced at least one other (nontaxonomic, nonthematic) relation, 82% of these other relations produced were solo. These results mirror those of Study 1, implying that thematic relations were less frequently produced *spontaneously* by children and often emerged as the result of maternal scaffolding.

### Relations in the Texts

In addition to coding mothers' and children's utterances, we also coded the texts of the books, for two reasons. First, all mothers read sections of the provided text during the course of the reading sessions. Thus, it is of interest to see what additional kinds of information children may have heard. Further-

TABLE 7

Mean Number of Relational and Single-Object Statements per 100 Sentences, in the Commercially Available Texts Used in Study 2

| Coding Categories | Farm Animals | Truck Book |
|---|---|---|
| Relational statements: | | |
| Taxonomic ................. | 25.59 | 12.90 |
| Thematic .................. | 53.22 | 63.62 |
| Similarity .................. | 22.22 | 21.86 |
| Contrast .................. | 8.00 | 3.57 |
| Other ..................... | 0 | 0 |
| Single-object statements: | | |
| Ostension ................. | 15.56 | 19.00 |
| Thematic .................. | 0 | 0 |
| Appearance ............... | 3.33 | 18.67* |

Note.—Asterisk indicates significant domain difference.

more, information provided in the text may not be reiterated by mothers in their spontaneous talk and so could be underrepresented in the data. Second, the texts provide a useful comparison or baseline. To the extent that mothers display different patterns from those found in the books, this demonstrates that maternal input is not simply following a script provided by the context.

A primary way to examine mismatches is to ask whether domain differences found in maternal speech are also found in the text. In other words, in the text, are farm animals and trucks treated differently? In order to perform statistical analyses on the text, we introduced variability by treating each page as a unit, in the same way that our prior analyses of the mothers treated each subject as a unit. This meant that, for each of the eight coding categories (five kinds of relational statements: taxonomic, thematic, similarity, contrast, and other; and three single-object statements: ostension, thematic, and appearance), we computed a score for each page separately: the number of coded instances on that page divided by the number of sentences. For example, if on a given page there were four text sentences, one of which provided a taxonomic relation, the score for taxonomic relations was 0.25 for that page. Because there were 15 pages in each book, we obtained 15 scores per book *for each coding category:* 15 scores for the farm animals book (one score per page) and 15 scores for the truck book (again, one score per page). For each coding category, these 30 scores (15 in each of the two domains) were compared by *t* tests.

As can be seen in Table 7, none of the relational statements yielded significant domain differences. However, single-object statements about appearance were more frequent for trucks than for farm animals. Thus, there were several telling mismatches between textual information and maternal speech.

Domain differences in maternal relations (more taxonomic relations for farm animals than for trucks) were not consistent in the texts.

Other mismatches concerned the relative frequency of different kinds of relations. In the text, similarity relations were as frequent as taxonomic relations; in maternal speech, similarity relations were quite rare. Likewise, statements about the appearance of individual items, especially trucks, were much more frequent in the text than in maternal speech. Thus, the distinctive pattern provided in maternal speech cannot be attributed to modeling in the text that mothers were reading.

### Summary: Relations, Study 2

Study 2 was conducted as a companion to Study 1. The question of interest was whether mothers would display the same patterns of results with ordinary books that, unlike the custom picture books of Study 1, were not artificially structured to highlight the contrast between taxonomic and thematic relations. In nearly every respect, the relations data in Study 2 mirrored those in Study 1. As before, we found that all mothers made statements explicitly relating two or more category instances and that relations tended to focus on taxonomic and thematic information (not similarity).

Similarly, taxonomic relations were disproportionately stressed for animal categories (i.e., farm animals vs. trucks). The pattern reversed when speech about individual objects was considered (i.e., mothers made more ostensive statements about trucks than about farm animals). Furthermore, when talking about farm animals, mothers provided more taxonomic relations than thematic relations; when talking about trucks, mothers focused equally on thematic and taxonomic relations. As in Study 1, and in contrast to claims of a thematic-to-taxonomic shift, children were no more likely than mothers to focus on thematic relations, in either a relative or an absolute sense. The primary difference between Studies 1 and 2 in the relations data concerned thematic relations, which unexpectedly yielded a domain difference in Study 1 (more for animals than for artifacts) but no domain difference in Study 2.

One possible objection to the domain comparisons in Study 2 is that the artifact book concerned a single basic-level category (trucks), whereas the animal book concerned numerous basic-level categories (farm animals). Thus, there was potentially a confound between domain (artifact vs. animal) and category level (basic vs. superordinate). However, despite its title, *The Truck Book* in fact included mention of a variety of distinct basic-level vehicles (e.g., trucks, buses, trailers, vans, campers, fire engines), several of which (trucks, buses, trailers) are explicitly listed as basic-level categories by Rosch (1975). Moreover, the analyses of maternal relations provide converging evidence that the books were similarly structured: in Study 2, the two domains produced equivalent proportions of basic-level taxonomic relations (66% for farm animals, 70% for artifacts).

Interestingly, the texts did not show the regularities found in maternal speech. Whereas mothers provided many more taxonomic than similarity relations, in the text taxonomic and similarity relations were equal in frequency. Moreover, the domain difference in maternal taxonomic relations was not matched in the text, in which farm animal and truck taxonomic relations were equally frequent. This is important for showing that the patterns displayed by the mothers were not simply modeled by the context.

Overall, the results of Study 2 demonstrate that the results of Study 1 cannot be attributed to the custom-designed books used therein. The use of custom picture books allowed us to frame more detailed questions about input but did not appear to bias the kind of input provided. Given this consistent pattern of input provided to 3-year-olds, we turn next to consider the input provided to younger children.

## STUDY 3: CUSTOM-DESIGNED BOOKS WITH 20-MONTH-OLDS

### Content of Relations

In all, 202 maternal relations (tallying types, not tokens) were identified. Taxonomic, thematic, and similarity relations accounted for 83% of these. As in Study 1, we predicted that taxonomic relations would be discussed more frequently than thematic or similarity relations, especially for animals. A 2 (domain: animals, artifacts) × 3 (relation type: taxonomic, thematic, similarity) ANOVA was conducted. Again, scores were divided by the number of utterances per speaker and domain. (For results, see Figure 7a.) As predicted, there was a significant main effect for relation type ($F[2, 28] = 22.63$, $p < .0001$). Similarity relations were significantly less frequent than taxonomic or thematic relations ($p < .01$), which did not differ significantly from one another. Also as predicted, there was a main effect for domain ($F[1, 14] = 15.78$, $p < .002$), with animals yielding over twice as many relation types as artifacts. The interaction was nonsignificant, indicating consistent domain differences for each of the three sorts of relations.

### Role of Similarity in Patterns of Relations

As in Study 1, we conducted a paired $t$ test, considering just the subset of items for which animal and artifact similarity scores overlapped. We examined the *sum* of all taxonomic, thematic, and similarity relations for these items (because, in the prior analysis, the only significant domain effect con-

63

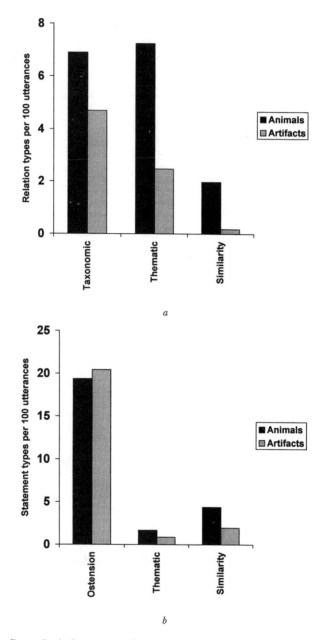

FIGURE 7.—a, Study 3, mean number of maternal relation types per 100 coded utterances, as a function of domain and content. b, Study 3, mean number of maternal statements about individual pictures, per 100 utterances, as a function of content and domain.

cerned taxonomic, thematic, and similarity relations combined). We divided these scores by the number of coded utterances produced for those items in each domain. On this comparison, relation types were still more frequent for animals than for artifacts ($M$'s = 16.11 and 7.44, respectively, $t$ paired [14] = 3.71, $p < .005$). Thus, domain differences in relations cannot be due to within-category similarity differences.

### Taxonomic Level

In Study 3, as in the two previous studies, the majority of taxonomic relations were basic level (87.5%), and, of the nonbasic relations, the majority referred to the animal domain (80%). Also as in Studies 1 and 2, the domain differences in taxonomic relations persisted even when only basic-level taxonomic relations were considered ($M$'s = 15.15 for animals and 6.97 for artifacts, $t$ paired [14] = 3.73, $p < .005$). Thus, the domain differences found earlier cannot be attributed to nonbasic levels.

We also conducted an additional analysis, controlling for both taxonomic level and within-target-category similarity. Specifically, we conducted a paired $t$ test, considering just the subset of basic-level items for which animal and artifact similarity scores overlapped (as above), and again controlling for the number of coded utterances produced in each domain. On this comparison, the summed score was still higher for animals than for artifacts ($M$'s = 15.02 and 6.84 types, respectively, $t$ paired [14] = 3.40, $p < .005$).

### Content of Statements about Individuals

As in Study 1, it is important to show that the results for relations (in particular, the domain effects) do not simply reflect how mothers describe individual pictures. In order to examine this issue, a 2 (domain: animal, artifact) × 3 (statement type: ostension, thematic, appearance) ANOVA was conducted. As before, scores were divided by the number of coded utterances per speaker and domain. (For results, see Figure 7b.) Unlike for relations, there were no domain effects when examining statements regarding individual items. There was a main effect for statement type only ($F[2, 28] = 81.97$, $p < .0001$). Ostension was much more common than either thematic or appearance statements ($p < .01$), which did not differ significantly from one another. Thus, patterns of relations are distinct from patterns of input about individuals.

### Pictures Linked by Relations

This section considers which pictures on the page the relations involved (target-category, contrasting-category, or thematic-associate pictures). Here, as in Study 1, we analyze only two kinds of relations: those involving exactly two pictures; those involving multiple pictures, *including* both target-category instances.

### Relations between Two Pictures

Each mother's relations linking two pictures were scored as to which pictures they linked. As in Study 1, tallies were adjusted to reflect the number of possible picture combinations, then divided by the number of coded utterances per speaker and domain. These scores were entered into a 2 (domain: animals, artifacts) × 4 (relation type: within target category, target plus thematic associate, target plus contrasting category, thematic associate plus contrasting category) ANOVA. This revealed a significant main effect for relation type ($F[3, 42] = 33.52$, $p < .0001$). As shown in Figure 8, within-target-category relations were more common than all other relations, for both animals and artifacts separately ($p < .01$). Neither the domain effect nor the interaction were significant. However, planned simple-effects tests indicated

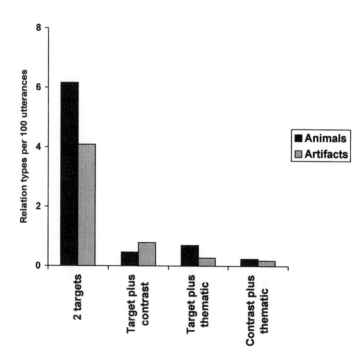

FIGURE 8.—Study 3, mean number of maternal relation types involving two pictures per 100 coded utterances, as a function of domain and relation type. (Scores were adjusted to account for the a priori probability of producing each type.)

that there was a significant domain difference among the within-target-category relations only ($F[1, 56] = 6.47$, $p < .02$).

### Role of Similarity in Patterns of Relations between Two Pictures

We conducted a paired $t$ test, considering just the subset of items for which animal and artifact similarity scores overlapped and for which the mean within-category similarity scores for animals and artifacts were equal. Again, we controlled for the number of coded utterances produced in each domain. On this comparison, although there was a tendency for mothers to produce more within-target-category relation types for animals ($M = 5.92$) than for artifacts ($M = 3.58$), this difference was not significant.

### Relations among Multiple Pictures

We also analyzed those relations linking the within-target-category pictures with either or both of the remaining two pictures: target-category pictures plus contrasting-category picture; target-category-pictures plus thematic picture; all four pictures. Scores were again divided by the number of coded utterances per speaker and domain. We performed a 2 (domain: animal, artifact) $\times$ 3 (relation type: target category plus contrasting picture, target category plus thematic picture, target category plus contrasting and thematic pictures) ANOVA. This yielded a significant effect of domain ($F[1, 14] = 6.71$, $p < .05$), a main effect of relation type ($F[2, 28] = 4.94$, $p < .02$), and a domain $\times$ relation type interaction ($F[2, 28] = 5.72$, $p < .01$). The interaction reflects the fact that multiple-picture relations were much more common for target-plus-contrasting relations in the animal domain (e.g., two birds plus a bat; $M = 2.10$ relation types) than for all other kinds of multiple-picture relations (ranging from 0 to 0.53 relation types). Thus, the only significant domain difference occurred for the target-category-plus-contrasting-picture relations ($p < .001$, simple-effects test).

### Statements Regarding Individuals

In order to make certain that the preference for within-target-category relations was not due to the salience of individual pictures, we examined the patterns of statements about individual pictures. Statements about individual pictures were tallied and adjusted as in Study 1 for the presence of two target-category pictures and only one contrasting and thematic picture each. We also divided by the number of coded utterances per speaker and domain to control for amount of speech. We conducted a 2 (domain: animal, artifact) $\times$ 3 (picture type: target category, contrasting, thematic) ANOVA. The analysis yielded a main effect of picture type only ($F[2, 28] = 8.92$, $p < .005$). There were fewer statements about individual target-category pictures ($M = 4.84$ types) than about thematic ($M = 7.00$) or contrasting ($M = 7.46$) pictures ($p < .01$). Thus, preference for within-target-category relations and domain effects was not due to the salience of target-category pictures or animal pictures.

## Correspondences between Content of Relations and Pictures Linked by Relations

As in Study 1, we examined the correspondences between the content of the relations and the particular pictures involved, in two ways. First, we looked at the content of within-category relations (relations linking, e.g., the two bats). We predicted that mothers would focus on taxonomic information when relating these pictures. Of interest is whether the domain differences found earlier (more within-category relations for animals than for artifacts) still obtain when examining just those within-category relations that mention taxonomic information. Second, we examined which pictures were the focus of mothers' discussions of taxonomic and thematic relations. Of interest here is whether, as in Study 1, thematic relations are used for a wide variety of picture combinations, including same-category items. Such a finding would again suggest that thematic relations may presuppose taxonomic information.

### Content of Within-Target-Category Relations

If mothers emphasize taxonomic categories, most within-target-category relations should be taxonomic in content. To assess this, we conducted a 2 (domain: animals, artifacts) × 4 (relations: taxonomic, thematic, similarity, contrast) ANOVA on the number of within-target-category relations divided by the number of coded utterances per speaker and domain. As predicted, there was a main effect for relation type ($F[3, 42] = 36.09$, $p < .0001$). Within-target-category relations were more likely to be taxonomic ($M = 7.05$ types) than thematic ($M = 0.07$), similarity based ($M = 0.46$), or contrasting ($M = 0.54$, $p < .01$). The latter three kinds of relations did not differ from one another. No other effects were significant.

### Taxonomic and Thematic Relations Analyzed by Picture Type

The data are presented in Figure 9. The majority of mothers' taxonomic relations were for within-target-category pictures (e.g., the two horses), whereas again thematic relations were spread more evenly across picture types. As before, mothers commonly invoked thematic relations for picture combinations that did not include the thematic-associate picture at all (36%

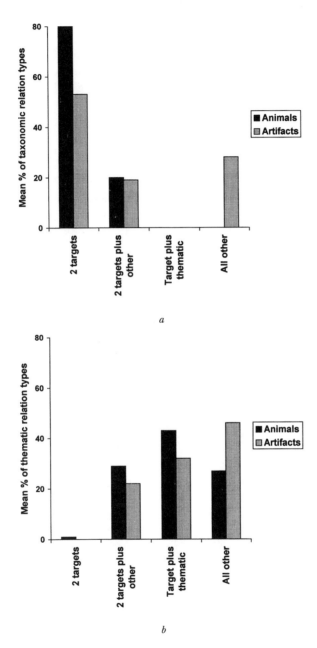

FIGURE 9.—*a*, Study 3, mean percentage of maternal taxonomic relation types as a function of domain and picture type. *b*, Study 3, mean percentage of maternal thematic relation types as a function of domain and picture type.

of animal thematic relations and 23% of artifact thematic relations were for such picture combinations).[8] Mothers also used thematic relations for picture combinations that included both target-category pictures (30% for animals, 22% for artifacts), again suggesting that thematic relations may sometimes build on taxonomic relations rather than conflicting with them.

We next report statistical analyses comparing taxonomic and thematic relations directly. As predicted, taxonomic relations were more likely than thematic relations to involve linking the two target-category pictures to one another (e.g., the two bats). Specifically, 67% of mothers' taxonomic relations but only 1% of their thematic relations were of this sort ($F[1, 14] = 104.95$, $p < .0001$). Furthermore, there was a domain effect: relations linking the two target-category pictures were more common for animals (41% of relations) than for artifacts (27% of relations). Also as predicted, thematic relations were more likely than taxonomic relations to involve linking one of the target-category pictures (or the target category in the absence of pictures) to the thematic associate (e.g., a bat with the cave). Specifically, 38% of mothers' thematic relations and none of their taxonomic relations were of this sort ($p < .05$, binomial test). These did not differ between animals and artifacts (43% and 32%, respectively, N.S.).

The third set of analyses examined how often mothers formed a relation that included the two target-category pictures as a subset (e.g., both bats plus the bird, both bats plus the cave, or both bats plus the bird plus the cave). In contrast to Study 1, there were no significant differences involving domain or relation content. It is interesting to note, however, that, overall, these relations were at least as frequent for thematic relations (26%) as for taxonomic relations (19%).

## Children's Questions and Relations

As in Studies 1 and 2, children's data were examined to discover what information children were eliciting and to probe for mother-child mismatches. Again, analyses were conducted to address two primary questions. First, we examined children's questions to determine whether maternal emphasis on taxonomic and thematic relations was spontaneous or was instead elicited by the children. The second major question is whether there were convergences or mismatches in mothers' and children's speech.

---

[8] These relations include all those referred to as "two targets" plus a subset of the relations referred to as "two targets plus other" and "all other." Because only some of the "two targets plus other" and "all other" relations exclude the thematic-associate pictures, the numbers provided here cannot be derived from the figure.

## Children's Questions

As in Studies 1 and 2, we coded all children's on-task questions. Questions that simply repeated part of an immediately preceding question posed by the mother were not coded further. Such questions accounted for none of the questions regarding the animal book but 12% of those regarding the artifact book. The remaining questions were coded along two dimensions: whether they referred to a single individual, more than one individual, or other; whether the content was taxonomic, thematic, appearance, or other. Coding agreement was calculated between the primary coder and a second coder, who coded three of the transcripts. Agreement regarding number of referents (single, plural, or other) was 77%; agreement regarding content of questions was 89%.

As in the previous two studies, if maternal relations were elicited by the children, then children's questions should have focused frequently on taxonomic and thematic information regarding multiple instances. Once again, this was not the case. The majority of questions were taxonomic and concerned an individual (84% for the animal book, 86% for the artifact book). Typically, these were questions such as, "What's this?" However, there were too few questions to analyze statistically (31 for animals, 7 for artifacts). Thus, as anticipated, children's questions focused on the names for individual items. Maternal focus on taxonomic and thematic relations was rarely elicited directly by these younger children.

## Content of Relations: Mothers and Children

Focusing on just the relational statements, we performed a 2 (speaker: mother, child) $\times$ 2 (domain: animal, artifact) $\times$ 3 (content: taxonomic, thematic, similarity) ANOVA to examine the possibility of mother-child differences in domain effects and/or content focus. As before, all scores were divided by the number of coded utterances per speaker and domain. The only significant effect involving speaker was a speaker $\times$ content interaction ($F[2, 28] = 3.75, p < .05$). Simple-effects analyses revealed that there was a significant speaker effect for thematic relations only ($M$'s $= 4.85$ and $2.06$ relation types, for mothers and children, respectively, $p < .05$). Mothers produced more thematic relations than did children, whereas there were no significant mother-child differences in the frequency of taxonomic or similarity relations.

## Children's Relations: Solo versus Scaffolded

As in Studies 1 and 2, we compared children's *solo* relations (those constructed by the child) with their *scaffolded* relations (those framed by the mother). For each child and each relation type (taxonomic, thematic, or other), we determined the percentage of relations of each type that were solo (as opposed to scaffolded), then calculated the mean for that relation type (excluding from consideration those children who produced no relations of that type). Thus, of the 12 children who produced at least one taxonomic relation, 99% of the taxonomic relations produced were solo. In contrast, of the five children who produced at least one thematic relation, none of the thematic relations produced were solo. Finally, only two children produced any other (nontaxonomic, nonthematic) relations; for these children, 42% of these other relations were solo. Although there were too few children to permit statistical comparison between thematic and taxonomic relations, the results again imply that thematic relations were less frequently produced *spontaneously* by children and often emerged as the result of maternal scaffolding.

### Pictures Linked by Taxonomic Relations: Mothers and Children

As in Study 1, we examined children's categorization errors by tallying how often children's (as opposed to mothers') taxonomic relations linked either (*a*) one target picture with another (e.g., two bats), which is appropriate for a basic-level relation, or (*b*) one or both target pictures with a contrasting-category instance (e.g., a bat and a bird or both bats and a bird), which is inappropriate for a basic-level relation. Because younger children produced so few relations overall, we combined the data from the animal and the artifact books and excluded from consideration those four mother-child pairs in which children produced no taxonomic relations. As predicted, children were much less likely than mothers to link both target pictures in their taxonomic relations (*M*'s = 43% and 76%, respectively, *t* paired [11] = 3.35, *p* < .01). Furthermore, children were more likely than mothers to link one or both target pictures with a contrasting-category instance in their taxonomic relations (*M*'s = 48% and 22%, respectively, *t* paired [11] = 3.45, *p* < .01). Thus, as anticipated, children often erred in determining the appropriate category boundaries for these picture sets.

### Summary, Study 3 Relations

The results of Study 3, examining maternal input to 20-month-old children, largely replicate the results of Studies 1 and 2. Again, mothers produced many relations (averaging 12.62 types per mother), focusing primarily on taxonomic and thematic relations. As in Study 1, thematic relations often included reference to taxonomic groupings, leading us to conclude that thematic and taxonomic groupings are not wholly distinct. Further support for this idea is that many of mothers' thematic relations (over one-fourth) were produced for picture combinations that included *both* target-category pictures. Finally, we obtained the same patterns of mother-child mismatch as in Study 1, with relatively more thematic relations for mothers than for children. The other notable result from Study 3 was the finding again of stable domain differences, with more relations (taxonomic, thematic, and similarity) produced for animals than for artifacts.

## DISCUSSION

A variety of measures show that maternal input stresses taxonomic relations among objects and does so disproportionately for animal categories. Specifically, mothers focused more often on taxonomic than on similarity relations, and two-picture relations linked same-category instances more often than any other two instances. (Note that the custom-designed books were created to control for the chance probability of linking any two pictures.) Moreover, taxonomic relations, relations linking same-category instances, and relations that included both same-category instances as a subset (e.g., both horses and the barn) all were more frequent for animals than for artifacts. These results held up over all three studies, using both specially prepared and commercially available books, and including input to both older (35-month-old) and younger (20-month-old) children.

The maternal focus on taxonomic relations does not mean that maternal input lacked thematic relations. On the contrary, we believe that it is mistaken to consider the two sorts of relations as competing with one another. For one reason, thematic relations were just as frequent as taxonomic relations in maternal input. For another, the domain difference in maternal taxonomic relations was often (i.e., in Studies 1 and 3) matched by a corresponding domain difference in thematic relations (in both cases, with animal relations more frequent than artifact relations). Thus, a rise in one kind of relation is not compensated for by a drop in the other kind of relation. Finally, in all three studies, thematic relations often presupposed taxonomic relations. For example, the thematic statement *Bats live in caves* rests on a notion of bats (as a category) and caves (as a category). In our data, mothers' relational statements were often of this sort, as can be seen by the frequency with which thematic relations made reference to both category members.

What does seem to be lacking in maternal input is explicit discussion of similarity relations. Perceptual similarity does not go unnoticed (witness the high frequency with which children's taxonomic relations erroneously included contrasting-category members). However, mothers rarely pointed out explicit relations on the basis of similarity alone. It may be that similarity relations are discussed less often because they are not deemed useful in conveying important category information to children or, alternatively, because they are salient even in the absence of verbal input. We return to this issue in Chapter VIII below.

The maternal distinction between animal and artifact categories, noted earlier, suggests that relations may provide children with an important source of information about category structure. However, it is important to rule out alternative accounts of the domain differences (i.e., to rule out the possibility that they can be attributed to factors other than category structure). The custom-designed books used in Studies 1 and 3 allow us to do so. The results cannot be attributed to familiarity (items in the two picture books did not differ in this respect), strength of thematic links (again, the two sets of items did not differ in this respect), similarity (control analyses were included that considered only those sets equated for similarity), or amount of speech (all analyses controlled for the number of on-task, intelligible [i.e., coded] utterances in each domain). The results also cannot be attributed to domain differences in preferred level of categorization as the results hold whether considering all taxonomic levels or the basic level only. It is also notable that the domain differences are specific to *relations* and do not extend to speech concerning individual objects. For example, although taxonomic relations were consistently higher for animals than for artifacts, ostension was no higher for animals than for artifacts. Similarly, although mothers linked the two same-category instances (e.g., two bats) more often for animals than for artifacts, they did not talk about the target-category instances *individually* (e.g., one bat) more often for animals than for artifacts. These differences, between relations and statements concerning objects taken individually, serve as a control to help rule out salience explanations of the domain effects. In other words, it is not the case that animals received more relations because mothers were more attentive to animal pictures overall.

Furthermore, we suggest that it is highly unlikely that the difference can be explained in terms of how much knowledge or information mothers have about animals versus artifacts. Recall that relations were coded as *types* per page rather than *tokens* per page. Thus, a mother could be counted as producing at most one relation of a given content type (taxonomic, thematic, etc.) for any set of pictures. For example, a mother who produced several different utterances taxonomically linking a given pair of pictures received no more credit than a mother who produced just one. This conservative coding system has the advantage of reducing (or even eliminating) knowledge effects given that mothers presumably know at least *one* taxonomic and thematic fact per category. Furthermore, mothers were provided with a rich set of information in the texts of Study 2 (the commercially available picture books), information that was largely invariant across domains. Thus, mothers had the opportunity to discuss, repeat, or elaborate on the information in the text, yet they again chose to emphasize taxonomic links more often for animals (specifically, farm animals) than for artifacts (specifically, trucks).

Finally, the commercial books in Study 2 help rule out the possibility that the custom-made picture books presented a preexisting bias toward taxonomic relations for animals. This bias could have taken three forms. First, the thematic choices for animals in Studies 1 and 3 were always artifacts, but the thematic choices for artifacts in Studies 1 and 3 were also artifacts. It was possible that this distinction was providing an extra level of contrast on each page of the animal books, leading mothers to make an animate-inanimate distinction and hence provide more discussion of biological categories as opposed to artifact categories. However, the commercial books in Study 2 help rule out this possibility: the truck book included people interacting with the trucks on 14 of the 15 pages, yet analysis revealed the same patterns of more taxonomic relations for animals than for artifacts. Second, in Studies 1 and 3, the custom-designed animal books were arguably more coherent than the custom-designed artifact books as only the former had a coherent domain that encompassed all pages (i.e., biology). This bias could conceivably have led mothers to talk more about taxonomic relations in the animal book. However, again the commercial books in Study 2 help rule this out because both books concerned two more coherent domains (trucks and farm animals) and the basic domain results still stand. Third, in Studies 1 and 3, the animals were typically more complex than the artifacts (more parts, movement, etc.), whereas, in Study 2, the domains were more comparable in terms of complexity, in that all the artifacts were complex machines.

A potential concern raised earlier was that the domain comparison in Study 2 may be misleading in that the artifact book was devoted to a single basic-level category (trucks), whereas the animal book discussed a variety of basic-level categories (farm animals). In response to this possible objection, in the summary of the results of Study 2, we pointed out that *The Truck Book* in fact discussed a variety of different basic-level categories (e.g., buses, trucks, trailers) and thus was similar in structure to *Farm Animals*. In other words, the word *truck* in the title of *The Truck Book* was used rather loosely, to refer to a range of heavy road vehicles. However, in future research, it would be valuable to control for category level more systematically across domains, taking into account both relatedness within a page and relatedness across pages within a book.

## Mother-Child Mismatches

In this chapter, in addition to examining maternal input, we also examined mother-child mismatches by focusing on (*a*) children's questions (and hence the sorts of information they elicited from their mothers) and (*b*) children's relations. In their questions, children primarily elicited names of individual pictures (e.g., "What's this?"), suggesting that maternal focus on relations cannot be attributed to requests for relational information on the part of the children. In their relations, children displayed patterns that were both similar to and different from those of their mothers. The similarities were twofold: children (like mothers) provided few similarity relations, and children (like mothers) showed some tendency to provide more relations for animals than for artifacts (in Studies 2 and 3, but not significantly in Study 1).

The major mismatch between mothers and children concerned thematic relations. Specifically, whereas mothers produced thematic and taxonomic relations with equal frequency, children produced more taxonomic than thematic relations. Thus, attention to thematic relations seems to *increase* from childhood to adulthood. This pattern is the reversal of the more usual thematic-to-taxonomic developmental shift that has been reported in the literature. In part, this finding may reflect the unfamiliarity of many of the thematic links portrayed in the books. Undoubtedly, children would have provided more speech about thematic relations had they been more familiar with or knowledgeable about the thematic links displayed (e.g., a spider and a web would be more familiar than a dolphin and a hoop). However, we do not believe that familiarity alone can account for the relative scarcity of thematic relations in children's speech. For one thing, many of the taxonomic relations were also unfamiliar, yet children still produced many taxonomic relations.

We suggest instead that taxonomic categories may be developmentally prior to thematic relations of the sort studied here. In the absence of prior knowledge, taxonomic relations may typically be more easily inferred from perceptual and contextual cues than are thematic relations. Although even young infants can identify same-category instances on the basis of static perceptual features (Eimas & Quinn, 1994; Quinn, Eimas, & Rosenkrantz, 1993), identifying thematic relations may require tracking the behavior of an individual across different contexts (e.g., a child won't know that a rabbit eats carrots until she observes the behavior). Thus, the "thematic-to-taxonomic shift" may largely reflect the difficulty of *superordinate* taxonomic categories (e.g., animal, vehicle) rather than of taxonomic categories more generally. To the extent that there are general shifts with age, the classic thematic-to-taxonomic shift may be characterized more accurately as a shift from taxonomic (basic level) to thematic to taxonomic (superordinate level). This argument is elaborated in more detail in Chapter VIII.

## IV. CATEGORY GENERALIZATIONS
## (INCLUDING GENERICS AND EXPLICIT QUANTIFIERS)

In this chapter, we examine how mothers make generalized reference to categories as abstract wholes. In contrast to the relations considered in Chapter III, which typically involved particular individual objects or animals (e.g., two individual horses; one horse and one barn), our focus here is on maternal utterances that refer broadly to most, all, or any category members (e.g., horses in general). Specifically, we focus on two different linguistic devices: (1) generic noun phrases and (2) the word *all* used as a universal quantifier.

Although generalizations occur with each use of a plural noun (Smith, 1992), generic noun phrases (e.g., *dogs* in *Dogs bark*, *a giraffe* in *A giraffe is an animal*, or *the hippo* in *The hippo is a four-legged beast*) are especially powerful means of conveying generalizations about shared properties of category members (Carlson & Pelletier, 1995). They do so in at least two ways. First, they involve properties that are definitional, recurrent, or law-like (Dahl, 1975) and true of the prototype. Thus, they are useful for making predictions and may be particularly important for conveying categories that have rich structure. Second, they make reference to objects as a *class* rather than objects as individuals (see Lyons, 1977). For example, *Dogs are friendly beasts* refers to the class of dogs rather than any particular dog or group of dogs. Indeed, some properties are true *only* of the class and not of *any* individual, such as *Kangaroos are numerous in Australia* (no single kangaroo can be numerous). Lyons suggests that generics can often be roughly translated as "generally," "typically," "characteristically," or "normally" (although not as "necessarily"). Unlike statements using *some*, generics invoke the entire category. Yet, unlike statements using universal quantifiers such as *all*, generics cannot be falsified by a counterexample and indeed need not even be true of most category members (Lawler, 1973, p. 329; McCawley, 1981). For example, *Birds lay eggs* is true of fewer than 50% of the category (excluding males and infant birds). Thus, generics convey properties that are associated with the category rather than with all or even necessarily most instances.

To put this another way, generic statements refer to *kinds* (Carlson,

1977): *Birds lay eggs* can be paraphrased as *Birds are a kind of animal such that the mature female lays eggs* (Shipley, 1993). Shipley (1993, 278) proposes that a generic statement such as this, "which presupposes the conceptualization of the class of birds as a single entity, should enhance the psychological coherence of the class of birds" for that speaker. However, there has been little, if any, psychological study of generics; nor have there been any reports of their frequency or distribution in adults' or children's speech. It is therefore interesting to note that various excerpts of parental speech provided in the developmental studies cited above are generics. For instance, in her examples of parental speech to preschool children, Callanan (1990) includes such generic statements as *They [hummingbirds] sort of make a humming sound* and *A mixer is what we use to mix things up in the kitchen*. Thus, generics may be a subtle but effective device used by parents to convey that members of a taxonomic category share properties.

Another way in which mothers might convey information about categories as a whole is to make explicit reference to all members of a category. The word *all* has a variety of functions, as can be seen in its different contexts of use (e.g., *all gone, all together now, all my children, all dogs*). Our focus is on the use of *all* as a universal quantifier, referring to the entire set of entities of a given kind (e.g., *all dogs*, meaning each and every dog, not bound to any given context). Universal quantifier uses of *all* are the most explicit and encompassing forms of category generalizations possible.

As noted in Chapter I, research on children's inductive inferences suggests that taxonomic categories are powerful guides for induction and that animal categories are especially so (Gelman, 1988; Gelman & Coley, 1990; Gelman & Markman, 1986; Gelman & O'Reilly, 1988). To the extent that maternal input accounts for children's patterns of inductive inferences, we would predict that mothers would often form generalizations (implicitly or explicitly) and would use them more frequently for the animal domain. Thus, we pose two specific questions: (*a*) How often do mothers make *implicit* generalizations using generics (e.g., *dogs bark*) as opposed to *explicit* generalizations using universal quantifiers (e.g., *all dogs bark*)? (*b*) Do mothers express generalizations more frequently for the animal than for the artifact domain?

## CODING

### Generics

In our coding of generics, we included statements as well as questions. Utterances that refer to specific instances (e.g., "They [referring to two specific eels] are long and skinny and look like snakes") were excluded. Utterances that did not refer to the target domain were also excluded (e.g., "Caves are dark" in the animal book because caves are inanimate). Statements such as "I like horses, too" were also excluded as they focus on the speaker rather than on the generic category. For Study 2, coding was restricted to those utterances referring to items that were the focus of the book (i.e., animals in *Farm Animals,* vehicles in *The Truck Book*) and the subject of the sentence. We did this because the books had many incidental pictures (e.g., people buying ice cream from the ice-cream truck) and we wished to maintain a clear comparison between the two domains. Each transcript was coded by one of two coders. Reliability was calculated by having both coders code a randomly chosen subset of the transcripts. Coding agreement was 98% in Study 1 (based on eight transcripts), 96% in Study 2 (based on five transcripts), and 94% in Study 3 (based on five transcripts).

## "All"

Two coders assigned each utterance containing *all* to one of three categories: (*a*) universal quantifier, referring to all members of the category, including those not immediately present (e.g., "I think chic———, roosters all have that thing"); (*b*) specified context, referring to all members of some specified subset of the category (e.g., "They all go in water, like fish," referring to all the animals on the page); and (*c*) other, including nonquantification uses (including unanalyzed expressions such as *all up,* e.g., "You eat them all up"). Coding agreement across the three studies was 85%.

## STUDY 1: CUSTOM-DESIGNED BOOKS WITH 35-MONTH-OLDS

### Generics

As noted earlier, for the animal books, generics were counted for animal referents only (i.e., generic statements regarding an inanimate thematic associate were not included). Thus, the probability of producing generics was theoretically higher for artifacts (for which all four pictures on each page were counted) than for animals. For the purposes of these analyses, however, we treat the two probabilities as equal, as the bias works against our hypothesis that more generics would be found for animals than for artifacts.

Mothers of 3-year-olds produced 117 generics, 96 for animals and 21 for artifacts (for a complete list, see Table 8). Of the 16 mothers, 14 produced at least one. Generics were distributed broadly across the animal categories, making reference to 17 categories from all 9 pages of the animal book. For all analyses reported in this chapter, each mother's raw score was adjusted to reflect the number of generics per 100 coded utterances for that book

TABLE 8

MATERNAL GENERICS, STUDY 1

| | |
|---|---|

Dyad 1
Sometimes bats live in caves.

Dyad 2
Do you know where bats live? In a cave.
Kitty cats love to unravel yarn.
Ants live underground.
And they [ants], when they're pushing the dirt up, it makes a little hill.
And they [chipmunks] eat the acorns.
Uh-huh, and what do eels look like?
They [eels] look like snakes, don't they?
A wok is how people in China cook.
Well, actually, a wok is how people in America cook like Chinese people.
And a compass makes circles.

Dyad 3
And they [seals] clap their hands together like this.
And they're [sharks] bigger fish.
They [sharks] jump through hoops.
A chipmunk's a little smaller than a squirrel.

Dyad 4
And eels are in water.
But they're [eels] not in lakes, like when we go swimming in lakes.
They're [eels] in oceans.
Remember, I told you cats like balls of yarn.
What's a clater [child's word for tongs] do?
And you can pick up food with them [tongs].

Dyad 5
They [anteaters] eat ants.
'Cause they [anteaters] have a long nose.
And they [anteaters] eat ants off the ground.
I don't know what they [aardvarks] eat.
Maybe they [aardvarks] eat ants, too, or bugs.
I think they [aardvarks] have long tongues.
Where do bats live?
Well, sometimes they [bats] do [live in the sky].
You know what, they [bats] actually live in caves.
And they [bats] come out in the sky at night.
And what do you think dolphins do in the water, with this [hoop]?
What do you think a dolphin would do with a hoop?
What do lobsters do?
They [lobsters] fish in the water?
And you can tell me what do you think goes in a toy car to make it go?
A compass tells us where we're at.

Dyad 6
For cars that's silly, though, right?
'Cause can cars can't go in your house?
Did you know sometimes bats live in caves, too?
You think kitties like to play with that [yarn]?
Do they [kitties] like to make a big string out of it?
They [dolphins] won't bite you?
They [horses] do [live in a barn]?

TABLE 8 (*Continued*)

Dyad 7
We use compasses to make circles.
Bats are little furry things that live in caves.
Do you think raccoons play with the cats?
And anteaters eat ants.
What do crabs do?
They [crabs] don't get eaten?
Eels are like snakes that swim in the water.

Dyad 8
And bats like to sleep in dark places.
They [bats] hang upside down when they sleep, isn't that kind of silly?
Well, they're [bats] nocturnal animals.
They [bats] go out at night because that's when they're awake.
They [bats] come out at nighttime.
They're [bats] kind of neat, aren't they?
I think anteaters eat ants.
And squirrels like to eat acorns.
They're [chipmunks] about that long.
They're [chipmunks] real cute.
Well, they [bats] like to sleep during the day for some reason.
They're [bats] called nocturnal animals, I think.
They [bats] sleep during the day.
And that's why they [bats] have to sleep in a cave.
And then, when the sun comes down and moon comes up, they [bats] come out and
    they fly around in the sky.
You don't have them [bats] too much in the city.
They [bats] like to live by rivers, too, and where there are lots of caves.
But they [bats] come out at night just because that's when they're awake.
They're [bats] just a different kind of animal.
Snakes like to live on—on land, it looks like.
They [seals] like to swim in water.
That's not the ocean, but they do live at—seals live in the ocean really.

Dyad 9
Um, sometimes toy cars don't have doors that open.
Sometimes birds can go in a cave.
They [chipmunks] love acorns.
Squirrels and chipmunks eat 'em [acorns].

Dyad 10
Eels live in the water.

Dyad 11
Oh, how come cars don't, don't fly?
What do you do with oots [child's word for boots]?
Is that something you do with oots [child's word for boots]?
Do dragons wear tennis shoes?
In banks, they have special places, or even in our own house, we could have a—special
    things called safes.
Yeah, but do you know how bats sleep, [child's name]?
How do they [bats] sleep?
Do you know how bats sleep?
Bats sleep upside down in the cave.
Bats don't fly around when the sun is out.
Bats are one of those animals that is awake all night.

81

TABLE 8 (Continued)

Do raccoons get to play with the—with balls of yarn.
And chipmunks are about this big.
Chipmunks are little bitty little animals.
They [chipmunks] don't spray people.
And do you know what dolphins do, [child's name]?
What—do you know what dolphins can learn how to do?
But eels never go on the land.
But eels only live in the water.
Because I think seals like to bounce balls.
And you know, sometimes they [seals] can balance them right in front of their nose.

Dyad 12
And what do we wear with shoes?
You wear socks with your shoes.
Cars used to look like that a long time ago.
What do chipmunks like to eat?
What do squirrels like to eat?
They [squirrels] like to eat nuts too.
And probably bird food if they [squirrels] had a chance.
Yeah, squirrels like to eat bird food.
What do sharks do?
Well, sharks eat all sorts of things that swim in the water.

Dyad 13
Do lobsters poop?
I imagine they [lobsters] do, yeah.
Do you know what batteries are for?
That's right, and they [batteries] make mechanical toys run, too, don't they?

Dyad 14
You know where seals go?
They [seals] jump in the water.
They [seals] go in the water and then get out of the water and go on the rocks.
[Do] you know what a dolphin does?

NOTE.—Dyads are numbered for the purpose of clarity.

(calculated separately for the animal and the artifact book). The adjusted mean for animal generics was 5.15 (SD = 3.76); that for artifact generics was 1.44 (SD = 1.52). Mothers provided significantly more generics for animals than for artifacts ($t[15] = 4.44$, $p < .001$). The frequency of generics and the marked domain difference are consistent with the interpretation that mothers indirectly convey to children which categories promote generalizations and inductive inferences.

### Similarity Control

A secondary analysis was conducted, counting generics only for those categories (seven animals, four artifacts) that overlap in similarity (see Chapter III). The adjusted mean for animal generics was 4.04 (SD = 3.62); that for artifact generics was 1.74 (SD = 2.64). On this measure, mothers again provided significantly more generics for animals than for artifacts ($t[15]$ = 2.76, $p < .02$). Thus, the domain differences in generic usage cannot be attributed to domain differences in perceptual similarity.

## "All"

None of the generics identified above employed the universal quantifier *all*. Mothers used the word *all* 23 times when reading the animal book and 27 times when reading the artifact book. None fell into the category of universal quantifier; 38% were classified as falling into the category of specific context, 62% into the category of other. Clearly, mothers were not explicitly instructing children about properties shared by all members of a category.

## STUDY 2: COMMERCIAL BOOKS WITH 35-MONTH-OLDS

### Generics

Mothers produced 63 generics, 55 for farm animals and 8 for trucks (for the entire listing, see Table 9). Of the 14 mothers, 13 produced at least one generic. Generics appeared for 13 different animal categories and were broadly distributed across the farm animal book. Mothers provided significantly more generics for farm animals ($M$ = 5.30, SD = 3.90) than for trucks ($M$ = 0.82, SD = 1.89, $t[13]$ = 4.01, $p < .002$). These results mirror those from the custom picture books of Study 1.

### "All"

Only two of the generics identified above were universal quantifiers ("I think chic——, roosters all have that thing," "Yeah, they [cows] all eat grass, I think"). In all, 56 instances of *all* were found (19 for the farm animal book, 37 for the truck book). Aside from the two universal quantifiers, five more (8.9% of all instances) were specified context uses (three for the farm animal book and two for the truck book), and the remaining 49 (87.5%) were other. Thus, as in Study 1, explicit generalizations to the entire category are extremely rare.

### Generics and Universal Quantifiers in the Texts

To what extent do the patterns of generic usage found in maternal speech simply reflect the information provided in the texts? If mothers are following a script modeled by the texts, then we should expect to find more generics in the farm animal book than in the truck book. In contrast, if moth-

TABLE 9

Dyad 17
What do rabbits eat?
And what else do they [rabbits] eat?

Dyad 18
What does a chick say?
Pigs like to eat corn?

Dyad 19
Do you know what kids are?
Those [kids] are baby goats.
Little rabbits are called kits.
They [ducks] don't always have people to feed them bread.
So they [ducks] have to find their own food sometimes.
Because they don't say that moms [sheep] have horns, just the dads [sheep].

Dyad 20
Yeah, but what do they [ice-cream trucks] sell?
Well, daddy chickens are called roosters.
And mommy chickens are called hens.
Do you know what baby goats are called?
Baby goats are called kids.
What's a chicken say?

Dyad 21
What's a turkey say?
They [tank trucks] carry things like gas, maybe, and chemicals for [unintelligible].
Oh, they [tank trucks] carry cookies, huh?
They [wreckers] pull cars that are broken down on the sides of the roads and stuff.

Dyad 22
No, what sound does a horsie make?
He [a horsie] goes hee, hee, hee, hee.
Do you know what sound a duck makes, [child's name]?
And what sound does a piggy make, [child's name]?
No, a piggie goes oink, oink, oink, oink.

Dyad 23
Do fire trucks, what do fire trucks do?
Farmers have tractors, and they use these.
Do you know what they [bookmobiles] do?
Roosters are man chickens, male chickens.
And sometimes cows give milk, don't they?
Cows eat grass and clover.
Did you know that little cows drink their mother's milk for a year?
Goats also give milk, did you know that?
Goats have milk.
They [male goats] use these to bump against each other, but I don't think he's mean.
That's just what goats like to do.
And baby goats are called kids?
Did you know that, um, donkeys like to kick?
Did you know that when a pig gets to be big, they're called hogs?
What's—do you know the noise pigs make?
Male sheep have horns, too.
They're [male sheep] called rams.

TABLE 9 (*Continued*)

Dyad 24
What do cows eat?
What's a sheep say?

Dyad 25
A calf is a baby cow.
Ducks have webbed feet.
OK, little ducklings stay close to their mother.

Dyad 26
Turkeys are bigger than chickens.

Dyad 27
What color are buses now?
What's a, what's a cow say?

Dyad 28
I think chic——, roosters all have that thing.
You know I think cows might just eat grass.
Well, I didn't know baby rabbits were called kits.
That's right, rabbits like carrots.
How do you think a goose honks?
What are baby ducks called?
They're [baby ducks] also called ducklings.

Dyad 29
Yeah, they [cows] all eat grass, I think.
No, cows are very gentle.
Yeah, horses eat grass.
Well, some horses—everything that has teeth can bite.
But if you hold it in a special way, they [horses] won't bite you.
They [horses] don't bite on purpose.

NOTE.—Dyads are numbered for the purposes of clarity.

ers impose their own bias in their generic usage, then the patterns found in spontaneous maternal speech should not be mirrored in the texts.

As in the previous chapter, we computed a score for each page separately: the number of utterances containing a generic noun phrase divided by the number of sentences. We compared the two books by treating each page as if it were a separate participant and comparing the two groups of pages (farm animals and trucks) by $t$ test. First, we considered the full set of generics, including both those that involved the entire category (e.g., *goats*) and those involving subsets of the category (e.g., *baby goats*). There were no significant domain differences in the frequency of generics in the farm animal book and the truck book ($M$'s = 66.77 generics per 100 sentences for the farm animal book, 50.48 for the truck book). Similarly, when considering only those generics involving the entire category, no domain differences were found ($M$'s = 35.44 generics per 100 sentences for the farm animal book,

28.81 for the truck book). Thus, the striking domain differences in *maternal* generics were not found in the texts (in maternal speech, 87% of generics referred to animals, whereas, in the texts, only 57% did so).

Statements employing *all* were not used at all in the farm animal book, and they accounted for a mean of only 3% of the utterances in the truck book, none of them used as universal quantifiers. The domain difference was not significant.

## STUDY 3: CUSTOM-DESIGNED BOOKS WITH 20-MONTH-OLDS

### Generics

Mothers of 20-month-olds produced 52 generics: 47 for animals and 5 for artifacts (for the complete listing, see Table 10). All eight of the mothers in the animal condition produced at least one generic; only three of the eight mothers in the artifact condition produced at least one. Generics referred to 14 different animal categories, representing all nine pages of the animal book. Again, mothers of younger children also provided significantly more generics for animals ($M = 6.05$, SD $= 2.50$) than for artifacts ($M = 0.85$, SD $= 1.50$, $t$ paired [15] $= 4.51$, $p < .001$).

### Similarity Control

As with Study 1, a secondary analysis was conducted, counting generics only for those categories (seven animals, four artifacts) that overlap in similarity. Each mother's raw score was converted to an adjusted score, reflecting the number of generics per 100 coded utterances for those 11 items (calculated separately for the animal and the artifact book). The adjusted mean for animal generics was 5.26 (SD $= 3.08$); that for artifact generics was 0.37 (SD $= 1.04$). On this measure, mothers again provided significantly more generics for animals than for artifacts ($t[14] = 3.68$, $p < .005$). Thus, the domain differences in generic usage cannot be attributed to domain differences in perceptual similarity.

### "All"

None of the generics discussed above included *all* as a universal quantifier. Indeed, mothers made very few statements employing *all* overall. Of the 16 mothers, 7 produced none whatsoever. Altogether, mothers made statements employing *all* eight times for animals and six times for artifacts. Of

TABLE 10

MATERNAL GENERICS, STUDY 3

Dyad 31
How does a snake go?
How's a snake go?
How's a kitty go?
How's a squirrelie go?

Dyad 32
What's a telephone say?

Dyad 33
Yeah, bats live in caves.
Bats have big wings.
What sound does a birdie make?
And cats play with balls of yarn, see?
And you know what squirrels eat?
They [squirrels] eat acorns.

Dyad 34
Anteater, do you know what an anteater eats?
An anteater eats ants from an anthill.
See how bats are different from birds?
They [bats] have bigger wings, and they have ears.
Uh-huh, and bats live in a cave.

Dyad 35
What do you say with a telephone, huh?

Dyad 36
What's a cat say, hm?
What's a squirrel say?

Dyad 37
You know what anteaters eat?
What do anteaters eat?
They eat ants.
Lobsters are in the water.
And squirrels love to eat acorns.
Do fish have tails?
What does a snake say?
And seals like the water, too.

Dyad 38
What's a kitty say?

Dyad 39
Mm-hm, and what does a horse say?
Bats, they live in the caves.
So bats and bears live in caves, sometimes.
What do, what do birdies say?
Do you remember what birdies say?
They [raccoons] come out at night.
They [raccoons] like to play at nighttime.
They [seals] kind of clap and make funny noises.
And they [seals] play with balls.
They [seals] put a ball on their nose.

Dyad 40
Is ice cold?
What noise does a car make?
What I . . . what sound does a car make?

TABLE 10 (*Continued*)

| |
|---|
| Dyad 41 |
| That's where bats live. |
| They [bats] live in caves. |
| I don't know what aardvarks eat. |
| Maybe they [aardvarks] eat ants too. |
| Right, they [lobsters] bite with those, don't they? |
| They [lobsters] pinch. |
| That's what seals do sometimes [bounce ball on nose]. |
| I think they [walruses] lay around mostly. |
| Zebras don't—usually don't live with horses, though. |
| They're [zebras] usually—they're out in the jungle. |
| Or sometimes they're [zebras] at the zoo. |

NOTE.—Dyads are numbered for the purpose of clarity.

these, none were universal quantifiers, three were specific context uses, and the remaining 11 were other.

## DISCUSSION

Mothers almost never made *explicit* reference to the inductive potential of categories in the form of statements using *all* as a marker of category-general or essential properties. Only two uses of *all* as a universal quantifier occurred in the entire corpus, across all three studies. Thus, it is implausible that children's category-based inferences can be explained as logical deductions from universal statements provided by mothers. To take an example from the literature, children's belief that dodos, but not pterodactyls, live in nests (Gelman & Coley, 1990) is most reasonably considered an *inductive* (not deductive) inference, extending beyond the information provided in maternal input. (As will be seen below, we consider inferences from generic statements to be inductive, not deductive, because generics allow for exceptions and thus do not apply to each and every category member.)

Nonetheless, generalizations in the form of generic noun phrases appeared frequently, exceeding 5% of maternal utterances about animals. Within the brief (15–20-minute) task, mothers produced an average of one generic every 3–4 minutes. Although linguists have noted that generics are of theoretical interest for their focus on definitional, recurrent, or law-like properties, these data are the first we know of to demonstrate that they commonly appear in maternal speech to children. It is especially notable in this context that this rate of frequency did not change over the age range studied (20–35 months). Despite the fact that young children's language tends to be focused on the "here and now" (Snow & Ferguson, 1977), mothers found it appropriate to make frequent reference to categories as entireties, abstracted away from any particular context.

The frequency of generics in maternal speech is consistent with the fact that generics are often used in induction tasks with adults (Osherson, Smith, Wilkie, & Lopez, 1990; Sloman, 1993, 1994) and young children (e.g., Gutheil & Gelman, 1997; Lopez, Gelman, Gutheil, & Smith, 1992; Waxman, Shipley, & Shepperson, 1991). In such experiments, information is often tied to kinds through the use of generics (e.g., *Robins have sesamoid bones, Fish breathe by taking water into their mouths*), yielding consistent category-based inferences. Thus, the use of generics to convey information about kinds appears to be a natural and very effective linguistic device.

Although the present studies did not examine children's *comprehension* of generics, we hypothesize that generics may serve two distinct functions for young children. First, and most obviously, generics may serve to teach children particular category-wide generalizations. From maternal generics, children can learn particular facts concerning animal vocalizations, habitat, diet, behaviors, etc. Because these properties are predicated of the kind as a whole, they may become more central to children's conceptual representations than they would had they been stated nongenerically. Furthermore, because these facts are stated generically (rather than as universal quantifiers), they may be particularly robust against counterevidence (e.g., *birds fly* allows for penguins, whereas *all birds fly* does not). Thus, even erroneous properties stated generically, such as stereotypes concerning gender or race, may be more difficult to counter and erase than erroneous properties stated absolutely.

The second potential function of maternal generics may be to indicate to children that a category as a whole is an inference-promoting entity, even beyond the particular properties mentioned in the generic statements. In other words, hearing numerous generic statements about a category may lead children to treat this category as a "kind," of which indefinitely many category-wide generalizations could be made. In short, we suggest that hearing generics may lead children to make inferences regarding the structure of the category. If this is true, then generics may serve this function even when the information is relatively superficial (e.g., "Little rabbits are called kits") or when little or no new information is provided (e.g., with such questions as "How do they [bats] sleep?") because the generic form itself implies that category members are alike in important ways.

A striking feature of maternal generics is that they were domain specific at both ages and in all three studies, appearing much more frequently for animals than for artifacts. The domain differences in generic usage cannot be attributed to familiarity (controlled across the two books in Studies 1 and 3), similarity (controlled in supplementary analyses in Studies 1 and 3), or amount of speech (controlled in all three studies). It is also unlikely that the domain differences can be attributed to lack of sufficient knowledge about the artifacts. Mothers certainly knew several category-general properties true of each artifact depicted (including its parts, function, thematic associates, and appearance) and mentioned many of these properties in reference to *particular* objects and contexts (as will be seen in Chapter V, where we discuss the numerous domain-specific properties referring to object use). Importantly, however, mothers typically failed to mention these properties in generic form.

Why, then, did animals elicit so many more generics than did artifacts? We interpret this result as reflecting conceptual differences between animal and artifact categories. Assuming that mothers construe animal kinds as more richly structured than artifact kinds (deeper similarities, greater coherence, etc.), it should be easier for mothers to conceptualize animal categories as abstract wholes and hence to use generics. Support for this interpretation can be found in the divergence between maternal input patterns and the models provided by the written texts of the books used in Study 2. Recall that the texts used in that study yielded many generics in both the farm animal and the truck domains. There were in fact no significant domain differences in generics found between the two texts. The fact that mothers nonetheless maintained a sharp domain distinction in their own generic usage provides strong evidence that the domain distinction arises from maternal conceptual biases rather than from information available in context. What is then interesting for the present discussion is that the domain difference in maternal generic usage is available to young children and may inform children's acquisition of this very same conceptual distinction.

We suggest that generics may be a "cryptotype" (Whorf, 1945), or covert category. Because the generic form is frequently used with one class of words (animate nouns) but rarely used with another (artifact nouns), it cryptically distinguishes animal categories from artifact categories. Whorf (1945) argues that cryptotypes are especially powerful because they are not consciously noticed and so cannot be explicitly discounted, nor can their implicatures be explicitly canceled. Certainly the patterning of generics is not the only linguistic distinction between animate and inanimate nouns found in English. Typically, only animates receive proper names (e.g., *George*), can be referred to with the pronouns *he* or *she,* or can be the subject of various verbs (e.g., *think, digest*). However, what is interesting about generics applying particularly to animates is the *meaning* that is then attached to the animate-inanimate distinction (Carlson & Pelletier, 1995), suggesting that animal categories (more than artifact categories) are particularly coherent and inference promoting. However, the present studies cannot tell us whether the animal-artifact difference that we obtained reflects a sharp distinction between animals as a class (including, e.g., amoebas and germs) and artifacts as a class (including, e.g., computers and robots) or whether instead there is a continuum or even an overlap between the two domains.

Although not all languages have a distinct generic construction (e.g., Mandarin), we would suspect that this pattern is not peculiar to English and would have analogous counterparts in other languages (Gelman & Tardif, in press). For example, in an investigation of Spanish verbs, Sera (1992; Sera, Reittinger, & del Castillo Pintado, 1991) found that the distinction between *ser* and *estar* maps roughly onto a distinction between inherent and accidental properties. Although English does not make the same distinction in its verb system, the propensity to use various kinds of quantifiers or generics may distinguish categories that promote inferences from those that do not.

One unexpected finding was the frequency with which generics were found in the texts of the commercially available picture books (Study 2). This result raises a host of questions, as yet unexplored, concerning how generics are distributed in written (as opposed to spoken) language and what role literacy plays in the use and distribution of the generic construction. As noted earlier, the high rate of generics in the truck book is important for ruling out an alternative explanation of the domain distinction found in maternal speech. Namely, the divergence between maternal input and the written text demonstrates that mothers were not simply following a script supplied by the book context. Moreover, this divergence implies that the cryptotypic difference between animals and artifacts, noted above, is not an obligatory grammatical distinction but rather a conceptual distinction imposed by speakers. Nonetheless, the divergence also raises a set of intriguing questions regarding the generality of the domain distinction outside a natural language context.

We suspect that informational books and encyclopedias will on the whole tend to be rich in generics because their purpose is to describe and explain phenomena outside any particular context. That is, informational books that are not historically rooted (such as biographies) tend to focus on general categories (e.g., breeds of horses, styles of music, kinds of diseases). However, we also speculate that books about animals and artifacts may differ in two major respects: (*a*) in how frequently they are informational (e.g., informational books about clothing or furniture may be less common than informational books about birds or fish) and (*b*) in how frequently they use generics in the context of fiction (for an example of a fictional text containing animal generics, see Dr. Seuss's *One Fish, Two Fish, Red Fish, Blue Fish*, 1960). In future research, it will be important to examine why and when domain differences in generic usage emerge.

# V. DOMAIN-SPECIFIC PROPERTIES

To this point, we have examined ways that mothers join two or more entities into larger groupings via relations, generics, and universal quantifiers. Thus, the analyses of Chapters III and IV focus broadly on the kinds of category structures mothers emphasize. In this chapter, we turn our attention to the *detailed content* of maternal speech, specifically, the information mothers provide that is especially relevant to one of two domains, either animals or artifacts (henceforth referred to as *domain-specific* properties). Domain-specific properties hypothesized for animals focused on self-initiated movement (Gelman & Gottfried, 1996), kinship (Hirschfeld, 1995b; Springer, 1992; Springer & Keil, 1989), psychological properties (Wellman, 1990), appearance-reality contrasts (Flavell et al., 1983), insides (Gelman, 1990; Gelman & Wellman, 1991), origins (Gelman & Kremer, 1991; Keil, 1989), explanations (Carey, 1985), and teleology regarding the self (Keil, 1992, 1994). Domain-specific properties hypothesized for artifacts included object use (Keil, 1989), teleology regarding another (Keil, 1992, 1994), and other-initiated movement. Finally, we coded utterances referring to other actions or behaviors as domain neutral.

Domain-specific properties are of interest for two reasons. First, they allow us to test whether mothers appropriately distinguish the content of the two domains (an important validity check of domain differences). Specifically, self-initiated movement, kinship, and psychological properties are (by content alone) more appropriate for animals than for artifacts; other-initiated movement and object use are (again, by content alone) more appropriate for artifacts than animals.

Beyond these literal differences in behaviors of entities in the two domains, there is a second reason for interest in domain-specific properties. Those hypothesized for animals have the potential to inform children about "deep" similarities among category members. Specifically, if maternal input is informing children about theory-rich properties in biological domains, we would expect to find statements such as *Birds and bats look the same on the outside, but inside they're different in ways you can't see* (appearance-reality contrast), *Dogs need blood and bones to stay healthy and grow* (insides), or *The bird came from an egg that grew inside her mother* (origins). In other words, mothers should describe those mechanisms and biologically relevant internal and/or theoretical properties that account for membership in richly structured animal categories. Thus, although appearance-reality contrasts, insides, origins, explanations, and teleology are relevant to both animals and artifacts (e.g., both animals and artifacts have origins that could be mentioned), we predicted that they should be especially frequent and detailed for animals if maternal input is scaffolding children's understanding of category structure.

## CODING

Actual examples of domain-specific property statements provided by mothers appear in Table 11. Each transcript was coded by one of two coders, who identified instances of eight animal-specific coding categories (appearance-reality, insides, origins, teleology [self], mobility [self], kinship, mental states/personality, and explanations), three artifact-specific coding categories (object use, teleology [other], and mobility [external agent]), and one domain-neutral property (other actions/behaviors), according to the following scheme:

TABLE 11

SAMPLE MATERNAL DOMAIN-SPECIFIC UTTERANCES, FROM STUDIES 1, 2, AND 3

| | |
|---|---|
| **Hypothesized for animals:** | |
| Self-initiated movement .... | I think they're [bats] just flying up in the air. |
| Kinship .................. | I'll bet you that's a mom [goat]. Because they don't say that moms have horns, just dads. |
| Psychological ............. | The goose is getting mad at the dog, see? |
| Appearance-reality ........ | These look like snakes, but they're called eels. |
| Insides .................. | Can you tell me what goes in a toy car to make it go? |
| Origins .................. | That's where we get our milk. The cows give us all the milk that we drink. |
| Teleology (self) .......... | Look at his nose. That's for eating ants. |
| Explanations ............. | That [cat] does look like a tiger, doesn't it? Because it has stripes. |
| **Hypothesized for artifacts:** | |
| Other-initiated movement ... | Because then they drive all your things down to your new house in the big truck. |
| Object use ............... | You put those [socks] on your feet. |
| Teleology (other) ......... | It keeps cement in there, and it rolls to keep mixing it when it's wet. |
| **Hypothesized to be domain neutral:** | |
| Action/behavior ........... | It's a clock that says ding. |
| | You know what, they [the squirrels] bury them [acorns] sometimes, too. |

1. *Movement* involves any reference to how the whole object traverses through space, either by itself (self-initiated) or with the aid of some other(s) (other initiated). If an agent is not explicitly mentioned and the verb is active, then it is coded as self-initiated.

2. *Kinship* includes any mention of familial relations (e.g., mother, father, baby, sibling) when used in reference to a picture in the book (e.g., "There's the mother cat, and there's the baby"). This code is not used for reference to the child's kin.

3. *Psychological* properties involve any wishes, desires, thoughts, intentions, or personality traits (including good/bad, nice/mean, etc.).

4. *Appearance-reality* statements were coded when both appearance and reality were stated (either in one utterance or across utterances), although the contrast itself could be implicit. Examples include *It's an X, (but) it looks like a Y; It's not X, but it looks like X;* and *It's an X shaped like a Y.* We *excluded* utterances such as the following because they were not sufficiently explicit: *It's like an X; It's an X, it's like a Y; It's an X, not a Y;* and *It looks like X.* Subordinate-level distinctions were also excluded (e.g., "These are special snakes that swim under water. And they're called eels").

5. *Insides* utterances include any reference to nonvisible insides (e.g., bones, motor, batteries).

6. *Origins* statements concern the initial source of objects (animals, artifacts, or plants), analogous to kin relations for animals (e.g., stating that a desk used to be a tree, that phones are purchased at a store, or that milk comes from a cow).

7. *Teleology* includes reference to why a feature exists by stating how it functions or serves a purpose. To be coded as teleology, a statement must single out a feature or part and mention its function. When the function helps the object itself, this is referred to as *teleology (self)* (e.g., a cat's tongue helping keep the cat clean). When the function does not help the object itself, this is referred to as *teleology (other)* (e.g., a cement-truck chute helps pour cement).

8. *Explanations* include any statement with *because* or some other causative (e.g., *so*).

9. *Object use* refers to what is done with something (implying an outside agent).

10. *Other actions/behaviors* involve anything that something does, apart from whole-object movement or object use. This coding category includes movement of a part, making a sound, living in caves, sitting, etc.

For Study 2, coding was restricted to those utterances referring to items that were the focus of the book (i.e., animals in *Farm Animals,* vehicles in *The Truck Book*) and the subject of the sentence. We did this because the books had many incidental pictures (e.g., people buying ice cream from the ice-cream truck) and we wished to maintain a clear comparison between the two domains. Intercoder agreement was calculated by having both coders code a randomly chosen subset of the transcripts. Agreement was 95% in Study 1 (based on eight transcripts), 94% in Study 2 (based on five transcripts), and 83% in Study 3 (based on five transcripts).

## STUDY 1: CUSTOM-DESIGNED BOOKS WITH 35-MONTH-OLDS

### Maternal Domain-Specific Properties

We calculated a set of composite scores, scores based on a priori predictions as to which coding categories should be higher for animals than for artifacts. One composite score (Animal Composite) included all the following coding categories, predicted to be higher for animals than for artifacts: self-initiated movement, kinship, psychological properties, appearance-reality, insides, origins, teleology (self), and explanations. Animal Composite scores were calculated for each participant and book separately by summing all utterances receiving any of these codes, then adjusting for the total number of coded utterances. A second composite score (Artifact Composite) included all the following coding categories, predicted to be higher for artifacts than for animals: other-initiated movement, object use, and teleology (other). Artifact Composite scores were calculated for each participant and book separately by summing all utterances receiving any of these codes, then adjusting for the total number of coded utterances. We had no predictions regarding other actions/behaviors. Altogether, then, each participant was given four composite scores: an Animal Composite score for speech about the animal book, an Animal Composite score for speech about the artifact book, an Artifact Composite score for speech about the animal book, and an Artifact Composite score for speech about the artifact book.

As predicted, the Animal Composite score was higher for the animal book than for the artifact book ($t[15] = 3.97$, $p < .001$). (Means are presented in Table 12.) Also as predicted, the Artifact Composite score was higher for the artifact book than for the animal book ($t[15] = 7.64$, $p < .001$). In sum, information provided about animals differed appropriately from that provided about artifacts.

We next examined individual properties to discover the source of these differences. Raw frequencies were adjusted to reflect the number of individual properties invoked per 100 coded utterances per speaker per book (these are summarized in Table 12). We conducted statistical analyses only for those properties that were mentioned by at least half the mothers or that were used in at least 1% of the total coded utterances. Such properties included self-initiated movement, psychological properties, appearance-reality, object use, and other actions/behaviors. As predicted, self-initiated movements were

## TABLE 12

MEAN NUMBER OF MATERNAL DOMAIN-SPECIFIC PROPERTIES PER 100 UTTERANCES (for all three studies) AND TEXTUAL DOMAIN-SPECIFIC PROPERTIES PER 100 SENTENCES (for Study 2), AS A FUNCTION OF DOMAIN

| | STUDY 1 | | STUDY 2 | | STUDY 2 TEXTS | | STUDY 3 | |
|---|---|---|---|---|---|---|---|---|
| | Animals | Artifacts | Farm Animals | Trucks | Farm Animals | Trucks | Animals | Artifacts |
| **Animal properties:** | | | | | | | | |
| Self-initiated movement | 2.78* | .00 | .12 | .79 | 9.44 | 22.81 | 2.36* | .18 |
| Kinship | .07 | .00 | 5.90* | .00 | 10.78* | .00 | .00 | .00 |
| Psychological | 1.20* | .00 | 1.79* | .00 | 10.00* | .00 | .34 | .00 |
| Appearance-reality | 1.36* | .65 | .24 | .19 | .00 | 1.33 | 1.14 | .18 |
| Insides | .00 | .58 | .00 | .63 | .00 | 2.86 | .00 | .19 |
| Origins | .07 | .06 | 1.33* | .24 | .00 | .00 | .00 | .00 |
| Teleology (self) | .15 | .00 | .13 | .24 | 2.22 | 3.33 | .21 | .18 |
| Explanations | .97 | 1.63 | 2.51 | 1.62 | .00 | .00 | .25 | .37 |
| Animal composite | 6.60* | 2.92 | 12.02* | 3.72 | 32.44 | 30.33 | 4.30* | 1.10 |
| **Artifact properties:** | | | | | | | | |
| Other-initiated movement | .00 | .21 | .00 | .04 | .00 | .00 | .00 | .35 |
| Object use | .07 | 8.35* | .62 | 2.38* | 11.89 | 7.29 | .48 | 4.07* |
| Teleology (other) | .00 | .52 | .51 | .56 | 2.67 | 6.29 | .00 | .00 |
| Artifact composite | .07 | 9.08* | 1.13 | 2.99* | 14.56 | 13.58 | .48 | 4.42* |
| **Domain neutral:** | | | | | | | | |
| Other actions/behaviors | 9.39* | .05 | 9.65 | 7.34 | 55.78 | 41.86 | 8.71* | .32 |

NOTE.—Asterisks indicate domain differences within a study.

mentioned more for animals than for artifacts ($t[15] = 5.95$, $p < .0001$), as were psychological properties ($t[15] = 3.01$, $p < .01$) and appearance-reality contrasts ($t[15] = 1.75$, $p = .05$, one tailed). Also as predicted, object use yielded higher scores for artifacts than for animals ($t[15] = 8.07$, $p < .0001$). Other actions/behaviors were also used more for animals than for artifacts ($t[15] = 7.56$, $p < .0001$). No domain differences were seen in explanations. It is of interest to note that three of these differences reflect literal differences between the two domains (self-initiated movement, psychological properties, and object use) and that one of the differences was unpredicted (other actions/behaviors). Only the appearance-reality contrasts provided evidence that mothers differentially stressed theory-rich properties for animals.

## Appearance-Reality Statements and Children's Naming Errors

Could the domain difference in maternal appearance-reality statements reflect a domain difference in children's naming errors? Specifically, if children make more errors when naming animals than when naming artifacts, this could lead mothers to explain the discrepancy between appearance and reality more for animals than for artifacts. To investigate this possibility, we coded how many of children's taxonomic relations erroneously linked items from contrasting categories (e.g., a bat and a bird; two bats and a bird). We found that the number of such relation types was identical for animals and artifacts ($M$'s = 1.875 per book) and in fact slightly higher for artifacts when controlling for the amount of speech children produced in the two domains. Thus, domain differences in maternal appearance-reality statements were apparently not elicited by children's speech.

A related issue is whether animal and artifact appearance-reality statements differ in their timing. Specifically, how often do appearance-reality statements directly follow a labeling error on the part of the child? For example, consider the following exchange, in which an appearance-reality contrast is provided to correct a child's naming error:

> Child: That's kangaroo. [Pointing to an aardvark.]
> Mother: Well, that looks like a kangaroo, but it's called an aardvark.
> Child: Aardvark.

At times, the appearance-reality statement not only corrects the child's error but also provides an opportunity to present further information, as in the following:

> Mother: Do you know what that one is?
> Child: Ummm.
> Mother: I don't know if you know what that one is.

> Child: That's a snake.
> Mother: It looks like a snake, doesn't it? It's called an eel. It's like
> a snake, only it lives in the water. And there's another one.

Appearance-reality errors that directly follow a naming error may be particularly salient and useful to children. In contrast, other appearance-reality statements were unprompted by children's naming errors, as in the following exchange:

> Mother: There's a white horsie and a brown horsie.
> Child: And a zebra.
> Mother: Right, a zebra. Looks like a horsie, doesn't it, with stripes.

Roughly half of mothers' appearance-reality statements followed a child's naming error (9 of 21 for animals, 6 of 10 for artifacts). This indicates that such statements can serve to correct children's errors, although this usage accounts for only a small proportion of maternal speech.

### Children's Domain-Specific Properties

In order to assess mother-child mismatches in domain-specific properties, we conducted two analyses, one examining the Animal Composite score and one examining the Artifact Composite score. Each was a 2 (participant: mother, child) $\times$ 2 (domain: animal, artifact) ANOVA. For the Animal Composite score, there was a main effect for participant: mothers produced higher scores than did children ($F[1, 30] = 14.70, p < .001$). There was also a main effect for domain, with higher scores for the animal book than for the artifact book among both mothers ($M$'s = 7.18 and 2.37) and children ($M$'s = 1.69 and 0.31, $F[1, 15] = 11.34, p < .005$). There was no significant domain $\times$ participant interaction.

For the Artifact Composite score, there was a main effect for participant: mothers produced higher scores than did children ($F[1, 15] = 40.22, p < .0001$). There was also a main effect for domain ($F[1, 15] = 49.41, p < .0001$) and a participant $\times$ domain interaction ($F[1, 15] = 39.92, p < .0001$). Mothers showed a larger domain difference between the two books ($M$'s = 0.12 and 7.69) than did children ($M$'s = 0.06 and 1.56), although the domain difference was significant in each group of participants (mothers and children) considered separately ($p$'s < .01, simple-effects test).

### Summary

Properties hypothesized to differ by domain were appropriately domain specific in both mothers' and children's speech. However, the majority of domain-specific properties produced by mothers and children concerned highly apparent properties (e.g., actions, behaviors, and object uses) rather than nonobvious or underlying properties (e.g., insides, origins). We turn next to Study 2 to determine whether these patterns are replicated with the commercially available books.


## STUDY 2: COMMERCIAL BOOKS WITH 35-MONTH-OLDS

### Maternal Domain-Specific Properties

As predicted, for the commercially available books, Animal Composite scores were higher for the farm animal book than for the truck book ($t$ paired [13] = 6.28, $p <$ .001; for the means, see Table 12). Likewise, Artifact Composite scores were higher for the truck book than for the farm animal book ($t$ paired [13] = 3.16, $p <$ .01). These results closely parallel those for the custom picture books of Study 1.

As in Study 1, we also examined individual domain-specific properties, conducting statistical analyses only for those properties that were mentioned by at least half the mothers or that were used in at least 1% of the total coded utterances. Such properties included kinship, psychological properties, origins, explanations, object use, teleology (other), and other actions/behaviors. The raw scores were adjusted to reflect the number of individual properties invoked per 100 coded utterances per speaker (calculated separately for the farm animal and the truck book). (The total counts for domain-specific properties are presented in Table 12.) Scores on each code for the farm animal book were compared to scores for the truck book. Four of these comparisons were significant: mothers discussed psychological properties ($t$[13] = 3.97, $p <$ .005), kinship ($t$[13] = 5.54, $p <$ .001), and origins ($t$[13] = 2.81, $p <$ .02) more for animals; they discussed object use ($t$[13] = 2.86, $p <$ .02) more for artifacts. All these differences were in the predicted direction. Three of these four properties were predicted on the basis of apparent differences between the domains (i.e., kinship, psychological properties, and object use, each of which is appropriate to either animals or artifacts, but not both). Only origins showed a domain difference above and beyond literal differences. That is, although both animals and artifacts have origins, mothers discussed animal origins more frequently.


### Children's Domain-Specific Properties

As in Study 1, to check for mother-child mismatches, we conducted an analysis examining the Animal Composite score: a 2 (participant: mother,

99

child) × 2 (domain: animal, artifact) ANOVA. There was a main effect for participant: mothers produced higher scores than did children ($F[1, 13] = 25.94$, $p < .001$). There was also a main effect for domain, with higher scores for the animal book than for the artifact book among both mothers ($M$'s = 9.71 and 3.57) and children ($M$'s = 4.36 and 0.21, $F[1, 13] = 7.19$, $p < .002$). The interaction was not significant. No statistical analyses were conducted on the Artifact Composite scores because only one such property was produced by a child in this study.

### Domain-Specific Properties in the Texts

Coding of domain-specific properties in the texts can be found in Table 12. Domain-specific properties constituted a higher proportion of the texts than of mothers' speech. There were significant domain differences between the farm animal book and the truck book with respect to two of the domain-specific properties, kinship and psychological properties, both in the predicted direction (more properties for farm animals than for trucks). These were the only domain-specific properties in the texts to show patterns found in maternal speech. Four other domain differences found in maternal speech were not found in the texts (origins, object use, and both composite scores). Thus, maternal differentiation of domain-specific properties cannot be wholly explained in terms of the texts provided.

### Summary

As in Study 1, nonobvious or underlying properties were rare in maternal speech. Also as in Study 1, both mothers and children discussed different sorts of properties for the two domains (in this case, farm animals and trucks). These differences by and large cannot be attributed to differences scripted by the two books as analyses of the texts of the books used in Study 2 found few domain differences. We turn next to Study 3 to examine maternal input to younger children.

## STUDY 3: CUSTOM-DESIGNED BOOKS WITH 20-MONTH-OLDS

### Maternal Domain-Specific Properties

The total counts for domain-specific properties produced by mothers of 20-month-olds (adjusted for number of coded utterances) are presented in Table 12. As in the previous studies, Animal Composite properties were mentioned more for animals than for artifacts ($t[14] = 2.66$, $p < .01$). Likewise,

Artifact Composite scores were higher for artifacts than for animals ($t[14]$ = 3.74, $p < .005$).

We then examined which properties were carrying these composite effects. As before, we conducted statistical analyses only for those properties that were mentioned by at least half the mothers or that were used in at least 1% of total coded utterances. Such properties included self-initiated movement, appearance-reality, object use, and other actions/behaviors. The raw scores were converted to an adjusted score, reflecting the number of individual properties invoked per 100 coded utterances per speaker. As predicted, self-initiated movement was mentioned more for the animal book than for the artifact book ($t[14]$ = 4.10, $p < .005$), as were other actions/behaviors ($t[14]$ = 5.12, $p < .001$). Also as predicted, object use was mentioned more for the artifact book than for the animal book ($t[14]$ = 3.65, $p < .005$). Two of these differences (self-initiated movement and object use) were predicted on the basis of literal differences between the domains; the third (other actions/behaviors) was not predicted.

### Children's Domain-Specific Properties

Comparisons between mothers' and children's domain-specific properties were not formally analyzed because only one domain-specific property was produced by the 20-month-olds: one child produced a single animal property; no artifact properties were produced. Obviously, then, the domain differences found in mothers' speech were not observed in children's speech.

### DISCUSSION

In the present studies, it was rare to find explicit talk about the nonobvious bases of categories. Although mothers mentioned domain-specific properties, they were primarily restricted to properties that literally distinguished the two domains (self-initiated movement, psychological properties, and object use). Other domain-specific properties that could be considered more theory relevant or nonobvious were almost never discussed (kinship, origins, and teleology). There was also little indication that such properties were more frequent for animals than for artifacts (e.g., talk about insides was focused on artifact parts, such as batteries; explanations were likewise somewhat more frequent for artifacts). The scarcity of such talk is striking given that the books in Studies 1 and 3 were designed to elicit discussion of nonobvious bases of categories, that children made many labeling errors, and that the mothers were highly educated and placed much emphasis on reading. The fact that mothers do not tell children about essences in a direct or explicit way suggests that essentialist beliefs evident in other developmental research (e.g., Gelman et al., 1994; Keil, 1989) are at least partially constructed by children themselves.

The one exception to this general pattern was that, in Study 1, appearance-reality contrasts were significantly more frequent for animals than for artifacts. This difference is particularly interesting given that the adult similarity ratings suggest that the appearances of artifacts were more deceptive (i.e., within-category similarity was somewhat lower for artifacts than for animals). That mothers find such contrasts more noteworthy for animals than for artifacts may suggest that mothers believe that it is more important to name animals accurately. Importantly, however, mothers did not explain the underlying *basis* of the appearance-reality contrast (e.g., nonobvious properties that differentiate snakes from eels).

As did the mothers, the older children (Studies 1 and 2) appropriately differentiated animals and artifacts in terms of the domain-specific properties provided (e.g., focusing on self-initiated movement and other actions/behaviors for animals and on object use for artifacts). Thus, by 35 months of age, children were knowledgeable about the content differences between the two domains. However, the younger children (Study 3) provided almost no domain-specific properties. This finding suggests that maternal input may be a factor in helping children learn the specific properties appropriate to each domain.

The patterns of input were highly similar across the three studies: mothers provided domain-specific information, but it tended to involve literal differences rather than theory-relevant or nonobvious properties. However, there were a few differences between the results of Study 2 (with commercially available books) and those of both Study 1 (with custom-designed books) and Study 3 (with younger children). Study 2 elicited much more talk about kinship (presumably because it displayed family groupings, unlike the books used in Studies 1 and 2). However, nearly all kinship references were minimal, simply making reference to kinship labels (e.g., "That looks like a mom turkey"), and none explained the biological bases of inheritance or kinship links. Study 2 also elicited less talk about the appearance-reality distinction, presumably because it did not include items with clear appearance-reality contrasts.

Another notable difference between Study 2 and the other studies was in maternal talk about "other actions and behaviors." In Studies 1 and 3, such properties showed marked domain differences (more frequent for animals than for artifacts), whereas, in Study 2, such properties were equally frequent across the two domains. We suspect that these properties reflect agency, the extent to which an item can be said to behave and perform actions on its own. In Studies 1 and 3, the artifacts generally are incapable of self-guided action or behavior, and thus events involving these artifacts tend to be mentioned as object *use* rather than as object *action/behavior*. In contrast, although the complex machines depicted in the truck book of Study 2 clearly require humans for their operation and use, they are more readily construed as having agency. Thus, for example, one mother in Study 2 said of a truck, "Look, and it picks up a big tree" (action/behavior), whereas a mother in Study 1 said of tongs, "They're for picking up ice" (object use). It may be that maternal focus on agency varies systematically with the complexity of the artifact involved. In any case, use of agentive language may be another subtle clue in maternal speech, providing information regarding the causal basis of object action/behavior as residing in either the self (agentive wording) or an external other (nonagentive wording) (see Gelman & Gottfried, 1996). However, because agentive language was not the focus of the present studies, these conclusions remain highly speculative and in need of further research.

# VI. GESTURES

Maternal gestures, like speech, can serve to focus children's attention on particular pictures in the books provided. By carefully analyzing the gestures (specifically, the nature of the gestures and which picture[s] are the focus of the gestures), we can make inferences regarding what sorts of information mothers highlight for their children. Thus, maternal gestures potentially provide converging evidence in a different modality, regarding the focus on taxonomic and thematic relations and also the role of domain in maternal input (as was done with the verbal information analyzed in Chapter III). However, gesture coding cannot be considered wholly independent of the relational statements reported in Chapter III as relational coding did make use of gestural information (e.g., pointing) when needed to disambiguate utterances (e.g., coders consulted the videotapes in order to determine the focus of such deictics as *this* or *these*).

Gestures are also intriguing in their own right, in part because they are more subtle and oblique than verbal statements. The indirectness of gestures makes them difficult for children to disagree with or counter directly (unlike verbal statements, which a child may explicitly contradict). Thus, in some respects, gestures may influence the focus of children's attention even more powerfully than speech. A final reason that gestures are interesting to study is that the distinction between gestures focusing on a single object and gestures focusing on two or more objects is a qualitative difference (see below), whereas the distinction between verbal statements about a single object and verbal relations is not. Thus, to the extent that we find similar patterns of results with gestures as with speech, this provides a strong confirmation of the distinction between verbal relations and single-object statements.

## CODING

As with picture coding of relations (see Chapter III), gestural coding was possible for the customized picture books only (Studies 1 and 3). Each videotape was coded by one of two coders, who identified instances of three types of gestures: points, links, and traces:

>*Point.*—Touching an individual picture on the page with a finger, a hand, or any part of the hand.
>
>*Link.*—(*a*) Directly dragging the finger from one picture to another;[9] (*b*) dragging the finger back and forth between two pictures, pointing back and forth between two pictures, or pointing to two pictures simultaneously.
>
>*Trace.*—Following the shape of either the whole object (its outline) or part of the object (e.g., the curve on a rolltop desk) with the finger by directly touching it on the page.

Coders excluded any gestures that appeared not to be part of the book-reading sequence (e.g., mother strokes child's hair, hand is used to support book), those that did not make reference to pictures in the book, and those that were occluded on the videotape by the book or the participants.

When a participant repeated a gesture to the same picture without the gesture being interrupted by another gesture (either by the same participant or by the other participant), the gesture was counted only once. For example, tapping a single picture several times counted as a single point; an elaborated tracing of the shape of a picture counted as a single shape trace. However, if a participant tapped a picture, traced it, then tapped it again, this was counted as two points and a trace.

Two independent coders, watching the videotapes with the sound turned off, coded each of these occurrences as well as the pictures they made reference to (e.g., a link between a horse and the barn; a point to the zebra; a trace of a horse). For each gesture, codes were counted as being in agreement if the two coders coded the same location (e.g., the same horse), type (e.g., point, trace, or link), and order in sequence (e.g., if one coder saw a point at the barn followed by a point at the zebra but the other coder saw a point at the zebra followed by a point at the barn, this would not be counted as agreement). Agreement was calculated by having both coders code a randomly chosen subset of the transcripts. Agreement was 83% for both Studies 1 and 3 (based on four participants per study). Gestures for Study 2 were not coded given the difficulties of reliably determining the focus of gestural links with the more crowded pages of these books.

---

[9] Hand sweeps (when a participant draws a hand over several pictures in one fluid motion) were decomposed into separate links. For example, if a mother swept her hand in an arc that started with the barn, continued to the zebra, and ended at a horse, this was coded as a link from barn to zebra followed by a link from zebra to horse.

*Missing Data*

During data collection, the camera operators attempted to capture on videotape all gestures toward the picture-book pages. However, some pages were not visible or not fully visible given the camera angle, the mother's position on the couch, and how the book was being held (e.g., only the back of the book could be seen). Therefore, we coded gestures only for those pages that were either fully or almost fully visible. We did not code gestures on a page if only a small subset of gestures on that page could be seen or if only one picture (of four) was visible. In order to correct for missing data, we multiplied each participant's scores within a given domain by the following index: 9/(number of codable pages). Because there were nine pages per domain, the index first determines the mean number of gestures per page (by dividing the total by the number of codable pages), then standardizes that number by multiplying by the standard number of pages (i.e., nine). For example, if a participant had one uncodable page, the index would equal 9/8; if a participant had no uncodable pages, the index would equal 9/9, or 1. The mean number of uncodable pages per domain in this study was 1.38 for animals and 0.94 for artifacts. Of the 16 participant pairs, 13 had three or fewer uncodable pages per book. Only one participant pair had no codable pages; this was for an artifact book. That pair's data were omitted from this analysis.

*What the Gestures Mean*

The gesture codes can be compared to the verbal coding in three primary ways. We view the gestural links as analogous to relational statements, points as analogous to ostensive statements, and shape traces as analogous to appearance statements. We elaborate on these interpretations below.

*Linking Gestures*

Gestural links draw comparisons between two pictures in much the same way as verbal relations do. Furthermore, some inferences can be made regarding the nature of the relation, inferences based on the pictures that are involved. For example, gestural links between the two target-category pictures can be assumed to emphasize some relation between taxonomically related instances; those linking a target-category picture and a thematic associate (or those linking a contrasting-category picture and a thematic associate) probably emphasize a thematic relation. Accordingly, if gestural links are analogous to relations and function to highlight richly structured categories, they should be most frequent for within-target-category pictures and for the animal domain.

### Pointing Gestures

Points appear to be analogous to ostensive statements in the verbal coding. For example, pointing to a cat draws attention to an object in much the same way that the statement *This is a cat* does (although of course the verbal statement provides crucial additional information regarding how the instance is to be named). Thus, as with statements regarding individual objects, we predicted points to be frequent, but not to appear more frequently for animals than artifacts, nor to appear more frequently for target-category pictures than for contrasting-category or thematic-associate pictures. In other words, we expected points to diverge from linking gestures in their distribution over pictures and domains.

### Tracing Gestures

Gestural traces serve to highlight the shape of the object being traced as well as to index maternal attention to individual objects.

We predicted that gestures would be relatively frequent when linking objects that are taxonomically related, that such taxonomic gestural links would be more frequent for animals than for artifacts, and that points to individual objects would show neither a taxonomic bias nor domain differences. Thus, our hypotheses mirror those for analogous verbal statements.

### Presentation of Results

In the following analyses, all significant effects were followed up using Tukey HSD procedures unless otherwise noted.

## STUDY 1: CUSTOM-DESIGNED BOOKS WITH 35-MONTH-OLDS

### Linking Gestures

If linking gestures are analogous to relations and function to highlight richly structured categories, they should be most frequent for within-target-category pictures and for the animal domain. The mean number of gestural

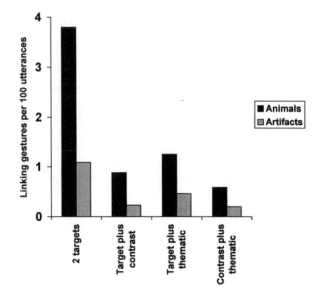

FIGURE 10.—Study 1, mean number of maternal linking gestures per 100 utterances, as a function of domain and picture type. (Scores were adjusted to account for the a priori probability of producing each type.)

links is shown in Figure 10. We conducted a 2 (domain: animal, artifact) × 4 (pictures: within-target-category pictures, target-plus-contrasting-category pictures, target-plus-thematic-associate pictures, contrasting-plus-thematic pictures) ANOVA. The dependent measure was the number of gestural links, corrected for missing data (as described above), and divided by the number of coded utterances by each speaker in each domain (to control for amount of time spent on each page).[10] Furthermore, the usual corrections were performed to equate for the possibility of producing each type (i.e., dividing by two for the target-plus-contrasting and target-plus-thematic pairs). This analysis yielded a main effect for domain ($F[1, 14] = 17.92$, $p < .001$), a main

[10] We divided by the number of utterances, rather than the number of gestures, in order to obtain a sensitive index of how much *opportunity* there was for mothers to gesture (i.e., the more a mother talks, the more opportunities she has to gesture). This correction also has the advantage of allowing us to determine whether mothers provide more gestures overall for one domain than for the other (a comparison that would have been impossible had we divided by the number of total gestures per domain). A final reason *not* to divide by the number of gestures produced by each mother is that some mothers produced very few gestures overall. Thus, if we had divided by the number of gestures, this would have resulted in some wide fluctuations in scores (e.g., if a mother produced only one gesture, then she would score 100% for whichever kind of gesture it was). Dividing by number of utterances presents more stable estimates.

effect for pictures ($F[3, 42] = 14.25$, $p < .0001$), and a domain × pictures interaction ($F[3, 42] = 7.37$, $p < .001$). As predicted, animal target-category links were more frequent than all the other kinds of links ($p < .01$). Simple-effects tests yielded significant domain effects for target-category links and for target-plus-thematic links, in both cases with animal links more frequent than artifact links ($p$'s $< .01$), but no significant domain differences for target-plus-contrasting or contrasting-plus-thematic links. Thus, as predicted, linking gestures mirror relational statements in their focus on taxonomic categories in the animal domain.

## Pointing Gestures

We predicted that points would function much as verbal statements regarding individual objects and so would diverge from linking gestures in their distribution over pictures and domains. We conducted a 2 (domain: animal, artifact) × 3 (picture: target category, contrasting category, thematic associate) ANOVA. The dependent measure was the number of points, corrected for missing data (as described above), and divided by the number of coded utterances in each domain (to control for amount of time spent on each page). Furthermore, the usual corrections were performed to equate for the possibility of producing each type (i.e., dividing by two for points to the target-category pictures, as there were two of each). This analysis yielded no significant effects. Points to the target-category pictures in the animal book ($M = 6.40$) were no more frequent than any of the other kinds of points ($M = 6.93$). Thus, mothers show no preference for pointing toward the target pictures, nor are their target-picture points more frequent for animals than for artifacts. As with the earlier analysis of verbal statements about individual pictures, this result provides an important control for comparison with mothers' gestural links, indicating that patterns of linking are specific to *relating* objects and not to gesturing in general. In other words, the finding that mothers provide especially many links for within-target-category animal pairs cannot be explained by positing that such pictures were overall more salient or interesting to the mothers.

## Tracing Gestures

Gestural traces provide information regarding the shape of the object being traced and thus are similar to pointing gestures in serving as an index of maternal attention to individual objects (in this case, perceptual features of individual objects). We conducted a 2 (domain: animal, artifact) × 3 (picture: target category, contrasting category, thematic associate) ANOVA on all traces (including those in the prior analyses). Traces of the target-category

GELMAN ET AL.

pictures were calculated as traces to both pictures divided by two. All scores were also corrected for the amount of speech per participant and domain. This analysis yielded a main effect for picture only ($F[2, 28] = 3.47, p < .05$). There were more traces of the thematic associate ($M = 1.91$ per 100 coded utterances) than of the contrasting category ($M = 0.97, p < .05$). Traces of the target category were in between ($M = 1.27$). Thus, in contrast to gestural links, with tracing gestures there was no tendency for mothers to show greater preference for animal categories. This implies that mothers' tendency to use linking gestures to stress taxonomic animal categories cannot be accounted for in terms of the salience of animal shapes taken individually.

*Mother-Child Comparisons: Linking Gestures*

To examine mother-child mismatches regarding linking gestures, we conducted a 2 (participant: mother, child) × 2 (domain: animal, artifact) × 4 (pictures: within-target-category pictures, target-plus-contrasting-category pictures, target-plus-thematic-associate pictures, contrasting-plus-thematic pictures) ANOVA. The dependent measure was the number of gestural links, corrected for missing data (as described above), and divided by the number of coded utterances in each domain. The usual corrections were performed to equate for the possibility of producing each type (i.e., dividing by two for the target-plus-contrasting and target-plus-thematic pairs). (For results, see Figure 10 above and Figure 11.) We examined only those effects involving participant. Surprisingly, there was no main effect of participant, indicating that mothers did not overall provide more linking gestures than children (when controlling for the amount of speech from each participant), perhaps due in part to the high variability of children's gestures. However, mothers did produce more linking gestures than children for some picture combinations, as shown by a participant × picture combination interaction ($F[3, 42] = 8.12, p < .0001$). Specifically, mothers produced more gestures than children linking within-target-category instances ($p < .02$). There were no mother-child differences for gestures linking any of the other picture combinations. There was also a participant × domain interaction ($F[1, 14] = 11.49, p < .005$). This indicates that mothers provided more linking gestures for animals than for artifacts ($p < .001$), whereas children showed no significant domain difference ($p > .90$).

## STUDY 3: CUSTOM-DESIGNED BOOKS WITH 20-MONTH-OLDS

As in Study 1, we coded gestures only for those pages that were either fully or almost fully visible. In order to correct for missing data, we performed

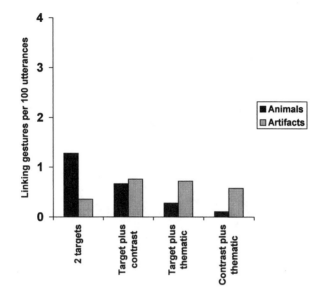

FIGURE 11.—Study 1, mean number of children's linking gestures per 100 utterances, as a function of domain and picture type. (Scores were adjusted to account for the a priori probability of producing each type.)

the same correction as previously described. The mean number of uncodable pages per domain in this study was 1.00 for animals and 0.75 for artifacts.

### Linking Gestures

We conducted a 2 (domain: animal, artifact) × 4 (picture pair: within target category, target plus contrasting category, target plus thematic associate, contrasting category plus thematic associate) ANOVA. The dependent measure was the number of linking gestures, controlling for nonvisible pages, corrected for the probability of producing each kind of gestural link, and divided by the number of coded utterances per participant and domain (see Figure 12). The ANOVA yielded no significant effects. However, a planned comparison examining just the within-target-category linking gestures revealed a significant domain effect indicating more gestural links for animals than for artifacts ($M$'s = 1.48 and 0.18, respectively, $p < .05$). Thus, mothers of younger children also differentially stressed gestural links for animals.

### Pointing Gestures

We conducted a 2 (domain: animal, artifact) × 3 (picture: target category, contrasting category, thematic) ANOVA. Scores for target-category pic-

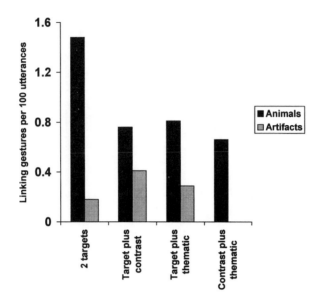

FIGURE 12.—Study 3, mean number of maternal linking gestures per 100 utterances, as a function of domain and picture type. (Scores were adjusted to account for the a priori probability of producing each type.)

tures were computed by tallying the points to each target-category picture and dividing by two. Again, we controlled for nonvisible pages and for the amount of speech (dividing by the number of coded utterances per participant and domain). This analysis yielded a domain × picture interaction ($F[2, 28] = 8.85$, $p < .001$). There was a domain difference for points to the thematic associates, with mothers pointing to thematic pictures less often for animals than for artifacts ($M$'s for the two domains $= 3.77$ and $9.09$ points, respectively, $p < .01$, simple-effects test). This pattern diverges from the domain difference in linking gestures noted above, suggesting that mothers' preference for animal as opposed to artifact within-category links cannot be attributed to the salience of each picture individually.

*Tracing Gestures*

We conducted a 2 (domain: animal, artifact) × 3 (picture: target category, contrasting category, thematic) ANOVA, again controlling for nonvisible pages, for the probability of producing each kind of trace and for the amount of speech. This analysis yielded no significant effects. Mothers produced an average of 3.91 traces per 100 utterances for the animals and 3.78 for the artifacts. This result, like that of the pointing gestures above, confirms that mothers' preference for animal as opposed to artifact within-category *linking gestures* cannot be attributed to the salience of each picture individually.

### Mother-Child Comparisons: Linking Gestures

Children produced too few linking gestures (only three in all) to permit comparisons with mothers.

## DISCUSSION

Gestures provided another subtle means by which mothers focused on within-category links. Specifically, mothers often produced gestures linking two pictures. Mothers of both younger (20 months) and older (35 months) children made more gestural links for within-category picture pairs (e.g., two dolphins) than for any other type of picture pair (e.g., dolphin and shark; dolphin and hoop). This result cannot be explained by positing that the within-category pictures were intrinsically more interesting than the other (contrasting-category or thematic) pictures because mothers revealed no preference for within-category pictures in their points or in their traces. Rather, gestural links seemed to be reserved primarily for indicating taxonomic category relations.

Consistent with the notion that linking gestures focus on richly structured categories, mothers of both younger and older children provided more gestures linking the same-category instances for animals than for artifacts (again, controlling for the amount of speech in each domain). Again, this result cannot be explained by suggesting that animals were intrinsically more interesting because there were no domain differences in the amount of points or tracing gestures (both of which focus on objects considered individually).

This greater focus on taxonomic category structure for animals than for artifacts largely mirrors the findings with the verbal relations of Chapter III. With both gestures and speech, mothers focused on same-category instances when linking more than one picture, provided more taxonomic links for animals than for artifacts, and displayed different patterns for objects considered in groups than for objects considered individually. Thus, in this context, gestures appeared to be conveying the same kind of information as speech. This result may not be too surprising when we consider that gestures during picture-book reading *complement* speech by disambiguating deixis (e.g., pointing to a picture to disambiguate a phrase such as *this one;* linking two pictures to disambiguate a phrase such as *these*). We would expect to find more divergence between gesture and speech during other sorts of contexts, such as storytelling (see McNeill, 1992), in which gestures to available referents will be less informative. We would also expect to find more gesture-speech mismatches when speakers are in a state of transitional knowledge (Perry et al., 1988). Thus, the present data should not be taken to mean that gestures generally tend to match up with speech, even during book reading. However, for present purposes, the parallels between these results and those of Chapter III are valuable for revealing the robustness of the patterns across different modalities.

Children's linking gestures appear to lag behind mothers' gestures and behind children's own speech in both frequency and informativeness. Children produced almost no linking gestures at the younger age and too much variability at the older age to yield significant domain differences. Thus, although gestures appear to be a subtle way that mothers convey information about category structure, gesture *production* does not represent a simpler or more accessible mode to young children. However, at this point, little is known regarding the extent to which children attend to, comprehend, or interpret gestures of the sort studied here. Given the clarity of patterns in maternal input, this issue deserves further investigation.

# VII. FAMILIARITY EFFECTS

The preceding chapters have focused on characterizing the nature of the input that mothers provide about category structure during picture-book reading. Another important question concerns *when* mothers provide the sorts of subtle features we have noted (e.g., relations, generics, domain-specific properties, and linking gestures), specifically the role of familiarity in predicting these input features. In the custom-designed books of Studies 1 and 3, we varied familiarity in order to observe maternal input in different sorts of contexts. The relatively familiar categories (e.g., *horse*) were included to determine how mothers *typically* talk about categories with their children, whereas the relatively unfamiliar categories (e.g., *anteater*) were included to determine how mothers *introduce new categories* to their children. Because past research focusing on parental talk has not typically varied familiarity (but see Callanan, 1990), our approach here is exploratory. We put forth two competing hypotheses: (*a*) Whatever information is provided when a category is first introduced may provide an important conceptual basis for further understanding. Thus, how mothers first establish a category may be an especially important time for them to convey the most fundamental properties. (*b*) On the other hand, it is also quite possible that mothers provide more important information about familiar categories, particularly because most parental speech concerns topics that are at least partly familiar to children (De-Loache & DeMendoza, 1987). Thus, it is important to include both familiar and unfamiliar categories in order to determine when mothers introduce important information about category structure.

## STUDY 1: CUSTOM-DESIGNED BOOKS WITH 35-MONTH-OLDS

### Mothers

To examine effects of familiarity, we conducted item-by-item correlations, for animals and artifacts separately, using mothers' ratings of their own child's knowledge of the words on each page. Thus, the familiarity ratings for each page were assessed by maternal ratings and averaged across all four pictures on the page (see Table 4 above). We used the composite score because many of the measures we wished to correlate with familiarity (e.g., relations, gestures) include reference to any of the four pictures on the page. Moreover, the four items on each page were presented together in a unified scene, and thus all four pictures on a page may have contributed to the familiarity of the page as a whole. Finally, the composite score provides a practical index that can be used consistently across the different measures described in the previous chapters.

To the extent that summing over the four pictures collapses over variation among the items on the page, we should simply be introducing noise (rather than systematic bias) into the correlations. However, we also consider the possibility that the relevant familiarity scores are those for the target and contrasting pictures (i.e., excluding the thematic associate), as these are the ones most typically linked in taxonomic relations. Importantly, when we correlate the composite scores that exclude the thematic associate and the composite scores that include all four pictures, the two sets correlate very highly: .98 for animals and .97 for artifacts. This again justifies our use of the four-picture composite score in the familiarity analyses.

The composite (four-picture) score was correlated with 17 measures for each of the animal and artifact books separately (see Table 13). Each of these correlations was computed using rank order (Spearman's rho). Overall, mothers of 35-month-olds tended to supply more information when picture sets were less familiar. Most of the correlations between maternal input and item familiarity (26 of the 34, or 76%) were negative ($p < .01$, sign test). For animals, there were two significant correlations with item familiarity, both negative, involving taxonomic relations and relations linking same-category pictures. Thus, mothers emphasize taxonomic information most for unfamiliar categories. For artifacts, there were four significant correlations with item familiarity, all negative, corresponding to thematic relations, ostensive statements about individual pictures, points to the contrasting-category pictures, and links between target-category pictures. For artifacts, mothers appear to emphasize both taxonomic and thematic information most for unfamiliar categories.

### Children

We examined familiarity effects for children in the same manner as we did for mothers, by conducting item-by-item correlations, for animals and artifacts separately, between the familiarity ratings of each item (mothers' ratings of their own child's knowledge) and each of the same measures included

TABLE 13

<small>CORRELATIONS BETWEEN MATERNAL INPUT MEASURES AND CHILDREN'S FAMILIARITY RATINGS</small>
(as Measured by Maternal Ratings)

| | STUDY 1 | | STUDY 3 | |
|---|---|---|---|---|
| | Animals | Artifacts | Animals | Artifacts |
| Taxonomic relations ..................... | −.74* | −.32 | +.46 | +.63 |
| Thematic relations ....................... | −.18 | −.71* | +.13 | +.18 |
| Same-category relations .................. | −.85** | −.48 | +.45 | +.18 |
| Target plus contrasting-category relations .... | −.08 | −.08 | −.67 | +.04 |
| Target plus thematic-associate relations ...... | −.36 | −.66 | −.03 | +.02 |
| Generics ............................... | −.33 | −.29 | +.13 | −.38 |
| Ostensive statements regarding individuals ... | −.65 | −.68* | +.62 | +.37 |
| Thematic statements regarding individuals ... | +.01 | −.11 | −.08 | −.26 |
| Appearance statements regarding individuals ............................ | +.07 | +.43 | +.02 | +.71* |
| Individual statements regarding target category .............................. | −.44 | −.28 | −.27 | +.84** |
| Individual statements regarding contrasting category .............................. | −.27 | −.55 | +.50 | +.19 |
| Individual statements regarding thematic associate ............................. | −.19 | +.02 | +.20 | −.14 |
| Points to target category .................. | +.17 | −.20 | +.23 | +.69* |
| Points to contrasting category ............. | .00 | −.68* | +.01 | +.50 |
| Points to thematic associate ............... | +.07 | +.15 | +.78* | +.33 |
| Gestural links between target-category pictures ............................. | −.19 | −.84** | .00 | ... |
| Domain-specific properties ................ | −.25 | −.09 | +.14 | +.78* |

<small>NOTE.—Positive correlations indicate that the measure occurred more frequently for familiar items, negative correlations that the measure occurred more frequently for unfamiliar items.</small>
<small>* $p < .05$.</small>
<small>** $p < .01$.</small>

with mothers. Two of the codes, generics and gestures linking target-category pictures, were used too rarely with artifacts (never or one time only) to be analyzed. This yielded 17 correlations for the animal sets and 15 for the artifact sets (see Table 14). Each of these correlations was computed using rank order (Spearman's rho).

In contrast to mothers, children tended to supply more information when picture sets were more familiar. Overall, most of the correlations (26 of the 32, or 81%) were positive ($p < .001$, sign test). For animals, there were five significant correlations with item familiarity, all positive, including thematic relations, relations linking same-category pictures, statements about the target-category pictures, points toward the target-category pictures, and gestures linking target-category instances. There were no significant correlations with artifacts. Thus, for animals, children were more likely to emphasize taxonomic categories and thematic relations for familiar rather than unfamiliar pictures.

TABLE 14

CORRELATIONS BETWEEN CHILDREN'S MEASURES AND CHILDREN'S FAMILIARITY RATINGS
(as Measured by Maternal Ratings)

| | STUDY 1 | | STUDY 3 | |
| --- | --- | --- | --- | --- |
| | Animals | Artifacts | Animals | Artifacts |
| Taxonomic relations ...................... | +.22 | +.48 | +.64 | +.62 |
| Thematic relations ........................ | +.70* | −.31 | +.47 | ... |
| Same-category relations .................. | +.88** | +.34 | +.88** | +.50 |
| Target plus contrasting-category relations .... | −.09 | +.31 | +.18 | +.08 |
| Target plus thematic-associate relations ...... | −.07 | .00 | ... | ... |
| Generics | +.05 | ... | +.39 | ... |
| Ostensive statements regarding individuals ... | +.57 | +.59 | +.75* | +.72* |
| Thematic statements regarding individuals ... | +.38 | +.12 | −.01 | ... |
| Appearance statements regarding individuals ............................ | +.56 | +.16 | +.78* | ... |
| Individual statements regarding target category .............................. | +.80* | +.42 | +.68* | +.56 |
| Individual statements regarding contrasting category .............................. | +.31 | +.34 | +.23 | +.48 |
| Individual statements regarding thematic associate .............................. | +.62 | +.39 | +.60 | +.82* |
| Points to target category ................... | +.77* | −.50 | +.15 | +.64 |
| Points to contrasting category .............. | +.58 | −.18 | +.48 | −.08 |
| Points to thematic associate ............... | +.18 | +.30 | +.51 | +.14 |
| Gestural links between target-category pictures ............................. | +.82* | ... | ... | ... |
| Domain-specific properties | +.26 | +.36 | ... | ... |

NOTE.—Positive correlations indicate that the measure occurred more frequently for familiar items, negative correlations that the measure occurred more frequently for unfamiliar items.

\* $p < .05$.

\*\* $p < .01$.

## STUDY 3: CUSTOM-DESIGNED BOOKS WITH 20-MONTH-OLDS

### Mothers

We again conducted item-by-item correlations, for animals and artifacts separately, using the familiarity ratings for each page (as assessed by maternal ratings and averaged across all four pictures on the page; see Table 4 above). Correlations between (a) the composite scores that exclude the thematic associate and (b) the composite scores that include all four pictures again correlate highly: .93 for animals and .77 for artifacts.

The composite (four-picture) score was correlated with each of the same measures included for Study 1 (excluding within-target-category linking gestures for artifacts, of which there were too few to analyze). (See Table 13 above.) Each of these correlations was computed using rank order (Spearman's rho). In striking contrast to the correlations reported in Study 1, mothers of these younger children tended to supply more information when picture sets were *more* familiar. Overall, most of the correlations (25 of 33, or 76%) were positive ($p < .001$, sign test). For animals, there was one significant correlation with item familiarity: a positive correlation with number of pointing gestures toward the thematic-associate picture. For artifacts, there were four significant correlations with item familiarity, all positive, corresponding to individual statements about one of the target-category pictures, appearance statements about individual pictures, pointing gestures to either of the target-category pictures, and nonobvious properties.

### Children

We examined familiarity effects in the same manner as was done with the mothers, by conducting item-by-item correlations, for animals and artifacts separately, between the familiarity ratings of each item and the same measures included in Study 1. However, several could not be analyzed because of low frequency (see Table 14). Altogether, we conducted 24 correlations: 14 for the animal sets and 10 for the artifact sets, each a rank-order correlation analyzed with Spearman's rho.

Even more than did the older children, 20-month-olds tended to supply more information when picture sets were more familiar. Overall, most of the correlations (22 of 24, or 92%) were positive ($p < .001$, sign test). For animals, there were four significant correlations with item familiarity, all positive, involving same-category relations, individual statements about the target-category pictures, ostensive statements about individual pictures, and appearance statements about individual pictures. For artifacts, there were two significant correlations with item familiarity, both positive, involving individual statements about the thematic picture and ostensive statements about individual pictures. Thus, 20-month-olds also tended to say more about familiar categories.

### DISCUSSION

An important feature of the picture books used in Studies 1 and 3 was their inclusion of items ranging in familiarity. We found consistent familiarity effects. For mothers of older children (Study 1), less familiar items tended to elicit more category-related talk and gestures than highly familiar items (including, for animals, more taxonomic and same-category relations and, for artifacts, more ostensive statements and gestural links between target-category pictures). If we assume that talk about unfamiliar items represents how mothers talk about new categories that their children have not previously encountered, this suggests that mothers are especially likely to focus on category relations while first introducing a new item. In other words, mothers seem to "anchor" (Callanan, 1985) new items by providing category information. One methodological implication of this result is that studies of how parents talk about familiar items (the most usual context for studying parental input) are incomplete and apparently systematically biased. In contrast, when examining *children's* talk, highly familiar items elicited *more* category and thematic talk than did less familiar items. Given children's more slender knowledge base, this last result was not surprising.

What was more surprising was that the mothers of the *younger* children (Study 3) focused especially on familiar categories, in contrast to mothers of the older children. This finding validates the assumption that maternal speech is sensitive to children's age (and presumably to their knowledge level and linguistic sophistication). It also demonstrates that the familiarity effects in Study 1 were not an artifact of certain items being more salient to the mothers. (Had it been an artifact, then the effect would not have reversed itself in Study 3.) However, it is still unclear how to interpret the developmental difference in familiarity. One possibility is that mothers employ different interactional strategies with 20-month-olds than they do with 35-month-olds (focusing on familiar entities at the earlier age and unfamiliar entities at the older age). A second possibility is that mothers are applying the same strategy with children of both ages, that of focusing on moderately novel items (which for the younger children are the familiar item sets but for the older children are the unfamiliar item sets).

More studies will be needed to determine which hypothesis has more merit. In any case, it will be valuable in future research to examine more broadly the influence of familiarity on parental input in order to discover whether these differences can be found in analyses of microgenetic change (e.g., on multiple readings of the same picture book; see Adams & Bullock, 1986; on microgenetic change, see Siegler & Crowley, 1991), to determine whether there are *qualitative* differences in the input provided for familiar and unfamiliar categories, and to examine whether the age-related differences obtained here are also found in other realms (e.g., parental explanations).

# VIII. GENERAL DISCUSSION

Human categories are impressively varied in function and structure. They range from ad hoc groupings that serve a single, arbitrary function (e.g., sorting shapes into red triangles and blue squares to suit the whim of an experimenter) to richly structured categories that are encoded in language, fostering inductive inferences and serving as the basis for biological reasoning (e.g., distinguishing birds from bats). These latter sorts of categories have at times been characterized as *richly structured categories, natural kinds, theory-laden categories,* or *categories with psychological essences.* They play an important role in a variety of cognitive tasks, including making judgments about identity, generalizing novel information, forming explanations, noticing correlated features, etc. (for reviews, see Gelman & Coley, 1991; Keil, 1989; and Murphy & Medin, 1985).

Research conducted over the past decade suggests that preschool children recognize the importance of richly structured categories. The evidence for this ability comes from a variety of tasks: Four-year-olds draw inductive inferences on the basis of category membership rather than appearances when the two are placed in conflict (Gelman & Markman, 1986, 1987). They report that internal, nonobvious parts can be more important than outward features for determining identity and salient behaviors (Gelman & Wellman, 1991; Keil, 1989). They maintain that, given a nature-nurture conflict, nature is more important (Gelman & Wellman, 1991). They distinguish between real animals and those in disguise, imputing nonobvious, biological features only to the former (Keil, 1989). They draw inferences on the basis of kinship rather than outward appearances if the two are placed in conflict (Springer, 1992; Springer & Keil, 1989).

Despite a wealth of studies detailing children's category knowledge, very little is known about *why* children expect that certain categories are richly structured, in the sense of sharing nonobvious properties and fostering inductive inferences, or *how* children differentiate among categories in terms of their capacity to promote such inferences. A critical piece of the puzzle would seem to be the nature of the input that children receive. Although parents provide much talk about categories to their young children, at present very little is known regarding what kinds of information are provided, beyond simple labeling (but see Callanan, 1985, 1990).

The present work characterizes maternal input in a middle-class U.S. sample, both to provide a descriptive database and to make inferences regarding the role of children's contribution. We selected a book-reading task because book reading is a common activity in this culture and provides a context in which information about categories is most likely to be imparted (Lucariello & Nelson, 1986). In Studies 1 and 3, the books were created to control for familiarity, within- and between-category similarity, and the likelihood of discussing various kinds of links among items. Study 2 provided converging evidence using commercially available picture books. Mothers were unaware of the purposes of the research, having been told merely that we were interested in parent-child interactions.

We organize this discussion in terms of two potential aspects of maternal input: as a database for children to consider and as a source of information to the researcher regarding mismatches between mother and child (Callanan, 1991). By examining input as a potential database, we can characterize when and how this talk potentially informs and shapes children's developing concepts. By examining mismatches between mother and child, we can suggest ways in which children's concepts, both errors and insights, are in part children's own constructions, not directly mirroring what they are told about the world.

## MATERNAL INPUT AS DATABASE

These studies uncovered much informative speech and many informative gestures regarding categories. The amount of information provided was surprisingly high, for both mothers and children as young as 20 months of age. The information that children received about categories included the following:

a) Statements about single objects (e.g., "That's a mom goat. You can tell because she has an udder");

b) Relational statements pulling together two members of a category (e.g., "These are special snakes that swim under water");

c) Generic statements referring to a general type rather than an individual (e.g., "Bats live in caves"), including statements that move seamlessly from referring to an individual to referring to a larger category of which it is part (e.g., "And this is *a seal*. And *they* clap their hands together like this" [emphases added]);

d) Gestural links (e.g., pointing to one category member, then dragging the index finger to point to another category member, or pointing to two category members at once); and

    *e*) Explicit discussion of domain-specific properties, including such nonobvious properties as appearance-reality conflicts (e.g., "He's a zebra. He kind of looks like a horse that's got stripes, though").

All the above are potentially informative about categories. For example, even simple ostensive statements (e.g., *This is a bear*) indicate that a certain entity is a member of a given category (*bears*). What varies is how detailed the information is (does it simply name the category, or does it provide additional information about specific features of the category?), how explanatory or essential it is (does it describe only features that are apparent, or does it introduce nonobvious, essential, and/or causal qualities?), and how broad its scope is (does it refer to an individual instance, or does it make reference to the category as a whole?). The most direct way of conveying which categories promote inferences or have essences would be to make statements that provide *specific features* that are *nonobvious and essential* while explicitly *referring to the entire category* (e.g., *All birds have sesamoid bones*). At the other extreme, it is possible to convey no category information whatsoever (e.g., pointing to a single object without saying anything, thus simply drawing attention to an individual object).

When considering this framework, we find that mothers rarely provide the kind of statement that would be most informative (explicit teaching about essential properties; e.g., *All birds have bird essences* or *Eels aren't snakes because all eels have certain kinds of parts inside that snakes don't have*). Not surprisingly, mothers never mentioned DNA, chromosomes, or internal bone structure. Perhaps more surprisingly, mention of insides at all was rare and was focused on artifacts more than on animals (e.g., batteries). Mothers in our studies did not use *all* as a universal quantifier, even though the word was plentiful in their speech. Although one might argue that it would be difficult for parents to talk about such properties (either because they did not possess the knowledge required to discuss these categories or because the vocabulary for talking about them would be too advanced to provide as input for a young child), we would suggest that such statements need not be arcane or pretentious.

Some of the justifications obtained *from children* in previous research provide a model for the kind of input that would be informative yet simple (Gelman & Markman, 1986, 1987; Gelman & O'Reilly, 1988). To quote from some 4–7-year-olds: "Snakes are a little bit the same and a little bit different. *Inside* they're the same." "That's the way rabbits are because that's how they are when they're born." "All flowers have nectar in 'em." "A snake has . . . lots of teeny bones, right? So it can wiggle. 'Cause if it was one long bone, it would just have to slide." "Every dog has the same stuff [inside]. . . . Just because [dogs] have different colors doesn't mean they have different stuff.'' Input of this sort was exceedingly rare.

However, mothers often stressed the importance of categories using more subtle devices: relational statements, generics, and linking gestures. Such devices go beyond ostension in two primary ways: by informing children about specific properties (of individuals or of categories) and by making reference to groups (as opposed to individuals). We discuss both these functions below.

### Information about Specific Properties

Although mothers often provided information concerning specific properties (roughly 30%–40% of their coded utterances included information beyond labeling), most such properties were neither essential nor nonobvious. They included actions and behaviors, object uses, thematic links, and appearances. Of these, actions/behaviors appeared primarily for animals, whereas object uses appeared almost exclusively for artifacts. These properties may thus have informed children about the sorts of everyday properties that can be inferred for each of these domains. We also speculate (see Chapter V above) that the form of such properties as agentive or nonagentive may also have provided children with indirect information concerning the causal basis of an item's action and behavior.

Interestingly, despite the salience of appearances for children's concepts, appearances were mentioned relatively infrequently when describing individual objects or when linking objects. Appearances were rarely mentioned even when the books included highly similar members of different categories (Studies 1 and 3). This result should not be taken to mean that appearances are unimportant to mothers. Rather, it may indicate that appearances are better conveyed through immediate perception than via language. For example, many perceptual properties are not readily described in language (e.g., the shapes that would distinguish a pig from a sheep from a cow). It is also important to point out that maternal input may focus children's attention on perceptual features implicitly. Specifically, providing different labels for two superficially similar items (e.g., a bird and a bat) may help serve to differentiate them perceptually, even without mentioning appearances directly. Similarly, labeling two apparently dissimilar items with the same name (e.g., *bird* for both a robin and a penguin) may help focus children's attention on featural similarities (e.g., beaks, wings).

In addition, mothers made fairly frequent mention of some nonobvious properties, most notably kinship, appearance-reality distinctions, and self-generated movement. Such statements were unelaborated. For example, mothers in Study 2 often mentioned kinship relations without discussing the biological basis of kinship. Similarly, mothers often acknowledged appearance-reality distinctions (e.g., "These look like snakes, but they're called eels"), but without going on to explain in depth *why* appearances are deceiving or what other features are more important than surface appearances. Nonetheless, despite the bareness of these statements, they may be informative. For example, appearance-reality contrasts could imply that certain (unspecified) qualities differentiate snakes from eels. It would then still be up to the child to figure out what form those qualities might take.

## Reference to Groups of Two or More Individuals

Mothers often talked about or gestured toward groups of two or more individual objects. Relational statements, linking gestures, and generics were all frequent means of linking an individual with a larger grouping. Relational statements and linking gestures appeared to serve similar functions. They disproportionately focused on taxonomically related individuals (e.g., two horses) rather than on individuals that were related thematically (e.g., horse and barn) or contrastively (e.g., horse and zebra). Moreover, the patterns found with relational statements and linking gestures were qualitatively distinct from the patterns found with statements about and points toward individual objects. Thus, by focusing on an item as one of a group, mothers may subtly convey taxonomic information.

The most dramatic instance of reference to more than one individual was the generic construction, in which the speaker pointed to one or two individual instances but talked about an abstract plural entity. For example, although there was only one chipmunk in the *Animal Friends* book, one mother referred to chipmunks as a plurality: "That's a chipmunk. And *they* eat the acorns" (emphasis added). Likewise, mothers sometimes shifted back and forth between the singular and the plural form: "Did you know when *a pig* gets to be big, *they*'re called hogs?" (emphases added). It is as if the speaker is saying (implicitly), "There is an entire class of things just like this one." We certainly do not yet know how children interpret these constructions, specifically, whether children interpret these statements as referring to the category as a whole. However, given the frequency of generics in the input, ordinary conventions of language use suggest that mothers assume that their children could figure out which larger class was intended by the utterance. As Clark (1992, p. 26) notes: "For a speaker to refer to a thing, he must be confident that because of his speech act the identity of that thing will become mutually known to him and his listener. It doesn't have to be mutually known beforehand."

It is noteworthy that, unlike universal quantifiers, generics cannot be falsified by counterexamples. That is, the presence of one penguin falsifies the statement *All birds fly* but does not challenge the statement *Birds fly*. In the extreme case, individuals may in fact make generic statements that are not true of most or all previously encountered instances (e.g., racial or ethnic stereotypes). Thus, generics are potentially more robust as input than statements explicitly generalizing to the entire category.

To summarize, the mothers we studied emphasized category relations, using a variety of verbal and nonverbal devices, but did not explicitly illuminate or elaborate on them. On the one hand, it is interesting that a variety of subtle devices were frequent even in input to the younger children (20-month-olds). On the other hand, it is interesting that the input was not very explicit given that our participant sample was highly educated and placed great value on books and literacy. One might expect a sample such as ours (primarily middle class, college educated, and sufficiently motivated to participate in research without compensation) to engage in relatively sophisticated talk with relatively high levels of discussion and explanation. The obtained pattern of results suggests that the input functions in a specific way: it implies that categories are important, without explaining their underlying or biological basis.

## Domain Differences

Given that animal categories are, on the whole, more richly structured than artifact categories (Gelman, 1988; Keil, 1989), we hypothesized that differences would be found in how mothers talk about animals as opposed to artifacts. As predicted, in all three of the present studies, pervasive differences were found between these two domains. First, as noted above, the content of maternal speech varied by domain: with animals, mothers talked about self-initiated movement and other actions and behaviors; with artifacts, they talked about object use. However, domain differences were not restricted to content: mothers focused more on categories for animals than for artifacts, in several respects. Mothers provided more relational statements for animals than for artifacts and related both members of the target category (e.g., both horses) more often for animals than for artifacts. This difference occurred not only in maternal speech but also in maternal gestures: mothers linked same-category instances in their gestures more frequently for animals than for artifacts. Particularly notable were the domain differences in generics, which were used much more often for animals than for artifacts in all three studies.

An important control for these domain differences arose in maternal speech and gestures about *individual* items: when talking about or pointing to pictures considered singly, no consistent domain differences emerged. In other words, the domain differences involved *category structure*, not just information about individuals.

Altogether, then, maternal input makes available a wealth of information about the importance of taxonomic categories and also differentially emphasizes the importance of categories for animals and artifacts. Thus, to return to the issue with which we began this section, we can conclude that maternal input does provide children with a rich, albeit subtle, database regarding category structure.

## MISMATCHES BETWEEN MOTHER AND CHILD

Surprisingly, there were relatively few mismatches between mothers and children. Like those of their mothers, the children's relational statements focused much less on similarity information than on either taxonomic or thematic information. Like mothers, children talked about actions and behaviors more for animals than for artifacts and about object use more for artifacts than for animals. The nonobvious properties that mothers of 20-month-olds provided (self-initiated movement for animals, other actions/behavior for animals, and object use for artifacts) were precisely those that 35-month-old children provided. However, there were also three primary points of mismatch between children and mothers during these sessions.

The first mismatch concerned category boundaries. In Studies 1 and 3, mothers typically used taxonomic relations for within-target-category (e.g., horse-horse) picture combinations; children as often used them for target-plus-contrasting-category (horse-zebra) or both-targets-plus-contrasting-category (horse-horse-zebra) combinations. In other words, mothers typically categorized the pictures correctly; children often made errors by grouping instances from different basic-level categories. Children's errors were expected given the design of the books, in which within-category similarity was on average only slightly greater than between-category similarity, where similarity was based on adult ratings (e.g., the dolphin and the shark were similar in appearance; the Snoopy-phone looked more like Snoopy than like a telephone). It was also expected that mothers would make fewer errors given their greater knowledge and given the printed labels that appeared in the books. Even if a mother was in doubt regarding the identity of the shark, she could consult the written word as a final authority.

Although unsurprising, the discrepancy between mothers and children as revealed in this analysis is important because it demonstrates that mothers had ample and explicit opportunities to explain to children why their classifications were in error. Thus, the data from Studies 1 and 3 represent, not only how mothers talk about categories, but also how they justify categorizations that are in dispute. It is noteworthy that, despite these opportunities, and despite explicitly noting differences between appearance and reality with some frequency, mothers almost never mentioned nonobvious properties, in-

127

nate potential, or other essentialist constructs when justifying the category membership of objects.

The second mismatch concerned domain differentiation. Domain differences in mothers' input were less consistently found in children's speech and gestures. Specifically, in Study 1, mothers provided significantly more relations for animals than for artifacts and significantly more linking gestures for animals than for artifacts, whereas children did not show these domain distinctions. This result is consistent with the suggestion that children start out with a general assumption that categories from different domains are richly structured (see Carey, 1995) and over time narrow this assumption to a subset of these categories. However, children in Studies 2 and 3 did not differ significantly from their mothers in amount of domain differentiation, when measurable (children produced too few linking gestures in Study 3 to conduct analyses).

Furthermore, in all three studies, children, like their mothers, mentioned different properties for the two domains (see Chapter V above). Such domain differentiation is consistent with other research with slightly older children demonstrating that, by 3–5 years of age, children separate animals and artifacts in important respects, including origins (Gelman, 1988), internal properties (Gelman, 1990), growth and metamorphosis (Keil, 1989; Rosengren et al., 1991), capacity for self-induced motion (Gelman & Gottfried, 1996; Massey & Gelman, 1988), and capacity for self-healing (Backscheider et al., 1993). Thus, overall, the mother-child mismatches concerning domains were modest and inconsistent, suggesting that, at least by 3 years of age, children are capable of treating the two domains as distinct.

The third kind of mother-child mismatch concerned thematic relations and was quite consistent throughout the three studies. Mothers focused on thematic relations more than did children, who typically focused instead on taxonomic relations. In other words, whereas children predominantly pointed out that pictured objects were the same kind of thing, mothers were just as likely to point out how pictured objects were related with respect to common goals, participation in a common activity, interaction with one another, etc. Additionally, even when children did provide thematic relations, they were often scaffolded by maternal questions. (In contrast, taxonomic relations were rarely scaffolded by maternal questions.) These results do not necessarily argue against a developmental shift in the relative salience of thematic relations, given that many of the thematic links depicted in the books would have been unfamiliar to these young children. That is, if the books had included more familiar thematic links (e.g., dog and bone, shoe and foot), we might have seen relatively more thematic statements among the children than among the mothers.

Nonetheless, the obtained developmental difference has two important implications. First, it suggests that children's thematic bias in prior research (e.g., Nelson, 1977; Smiley & Brown, 1979) may not be so surprising given how often mothers talk about and encourage such links. Second, and more speculatively, it also suggests that children's attention to thematic links may build on their appreciation of taxonomic links rather than competing with them (for alternative critiques of the thematic-to-taxonomic shift, see also Blewitt & Toppino, 1991; Lin, 1996; Lucariello, Kyratzis, & Nelson, 1992; and Waxman & Namy, 1997). The argument rests on two independent points: (a) that most thematic relations presuppose a taxonomic relation and (b) that taxonomic relations may be more easily inferred, in the absence of previous direct knowledge, from perceptual and contextual cues. We briefly detail these suggestions below.

The claim that thematic relations often presuppose a taxonomic relation rests on the distinction between objects as individuals and objects as category members. Thematic relations can be of either sort. *This [individual] blouse matches this [individual] skirt* rests on a notion of the blouse and the skirt as individuals, not necessarily representative of blouses and skirts as categories (after all, blouses in general typically do not match skirts in general). In contrast, *Bats live in caves* rests on a notion of bats (as a category) and caves (as a category). In this latter case, the thematic link presupposes the taxonomic categories *bat* and *cave*. Even a statement such as *This bat lives in a cave*, which refers to an individual bat and an individual cave, is likely to draw on taxonomic knowledge about bats and caves in general. We further suggest that thematic relations that people find salient, particularly those that psychologists have studied developmentally (e.g., spider-web, cow-milk; see Markman & Hutchinson, 1984; Smiley & Brown, 1979), tend to be of the second sort: resting on notions of objects as category members. If this conjecture turns out to be true, then this would mean that most thematic relations presuppose taxonomic relations and that taxonomic relations are developmentally primary.

The second suggestion is that, in the absence of direct knowledge, it may be easier to infer taxonomic (as opposed to thematic) relations on the basis of available perceptual and contextual cues. Our perceptual system seems designed to notice featural similarities in ways that permit identification of same-category instances as early as 3 or 4 months of age (Eimas & Quinn, 1994; Quinn, Eimas, & Rosenkrantz, 1993). Furthermore, words are mapped onto taxonomic categories as early as the first year of life (Balaban & Waxman, 1997; Waxman & Hall, 1993; Waxman & Markow, 1995). Identification of thematic relations may require tracking the behavior of an individual over time (e.g., a child will not know that a rabbit eats carrots until she either observes the rabbit in that context or is told by others about the thematic link), and tracking an instance over time may be more difficult than noting the features of a static object (Oakes & Madole, 1996). Moreover, identifying *new* instances of a thematic relation logically requires the use of categories:

after learning that a particular rabbit eats a particular carrot, to predict that another rabbit will eat a carrot entails categorizing different instances of rabbits (and of carrots) as alike.

Given these analyses, why have developmental psychologists found such rich evidence for a thematic-to-taxonomic shift (see Markman & Hutchinson, 1984; Nelson, 1977; Smiley & Brown, 1979)? The answer may lie in part in the kinds of taxonomic categories tested: some studies have focused on superordinate-level categories (such as *animal* or *vehicle*) rather than on the basic-level categories examined in the present studies. There is already an extensive literature documenting the relative difficulty of the superordinate level relative to the basic level (Golinkoff, Shuff-Bailey, Olguin, & Ruan, 1995; Markman & Callanan, 1984). Thus, to the extent that there are general shifts with age, the classic "thematic-to-taxonomic shift" may be characterized more accurately as a shift from taxonomic (basic level) to thematic to taxonomic (superordinate level).

In addition to the mother-child mismatches described above, we also found a number of discrepancies between the maternal speech documented in this *Monograph* and what one might expect to find in maternal speech on the basis of children's performance on prior experimental tasks presented in the literature. Specifically, although children have a rich set of beliefs about insides, teleology, and origins (see Gelman & Wellman, 1991; Keil, 1994), mothers provided almost no corresponding input about these topics. We obtained no evidence that these understandings are being tutored by mothers, thus suggesting that children may be constructing these beliefs largely on the basis of indirect evidence. This is particularly striking given that Studies 1 and 3 used books that were specifically designed to focus mothers on category boundaries and deceptive appearances. From other evidence (maternal appearance-reality statements and boundary errors in children's relational statements), we know that the specially prepared picture books succeeded in providing appearance-reality conflicts; nonetheless, these books did not foster much discussion of nonobvious properties.

## IMPLICATIONS FOR ACQUISITION

We turn now to the issue of what the input implies about acquisition. Simply put, what are the effects of maternal input on children's concept learning? The present studies were not designed to answer this question directly, having neither (*a*) measured children's comprehension/interpretation of features of maternal input nor (*b*) found sufficient variation to determine causal implications at the level of individual differences. However, there are three notable features of the input that provide relevant clues.

First, as noted earlier, the input can be characterized as implicit rather than explicit. Mothers *imply* that certain objects go together, via gestures and relational statements; they *imply* that certain categories have agency, via facts about everyday properties (actions, behaviors, functions); they *imply* that certain categories promote inferences, via generics. They do not *explicitly state* that categories are richly structured, via talk about nonobvious essences, about causal agency, or about properties shared by all category members. Second, and relatedly, the input (at least at this young age) focuses on inductive potential and shared features rather than on detailed biological facts. Indeed, mothers stress such shared features and inductive potential even with unfamiliar categories for which children have minimal knowledge. Third, the input clearly distinguishes categories of different sorts (specifically, animal and artifact categories), even controlling for features of the individual objects (similarity, familiarity, thematic relatedness).

Together, these findings suggest that, if maternal input exerts an influence, it is of two sorts: (*a*) mothers teach children about kinds, not about essences, and (*b*) mothers help children identify which categories are richly structured. We briefly expand these points below.

*Kinds versus Essences*

The present data do not support a developmental story that says that children build up beliefs about category structure from particular facts about internal, nonobvious similarities shared by particular instances of particular categories. Rather, it is more likely that children have a general understanding that categories are important, inference-promoting, richly structured entities ("kinds"; see Wierzbicka, 1994), a "skeletal" understanding (Gelman, 1990) that gets filled in with specifics only later (see Medin's, 1989, "essence placeholder" notion). In light of these data, it is useful to distinguish between "kind" information and "essentialist" information. Kind information conveys the notion that different instances cohere into a richly structured, inference-promoting category (a "natural kind"; Schwartz, 1977, 1979; see also Gopnik & Meltzoff, 1997), without explaining the basis of the category or what nonobvious substance or property holds the category together. In contrast, essentialist information conveys the category essence, be it material substance (e.g., DNA) or something else (e.g., soul, vital force).

The input characterized in these studies is of the first sort: it conveys the notion that animals are sorted into kinds, but it does not describe or explain the basis of kind membership. Our findings are therefore consistent with Simons and Keil's (1995) notion that children may proceed from abstract to concrete rather than the reverse. Maternal input provides an abstract framework in which taxonomic categories (particularly taxonomic animal categories) are important but little specific information regarding precisely how or why.

## Identifying Richly Structured Categories

Maternal input also plausibly helps children figure out *which* categories are richly structured. The input from mothers in the present studies is redundantly informative about distinctions between animals and artifacts. Moreover, these patterns in the input are present even in speech to 20-month-old children. The suggestion that subtle features of maternal input exert an influence could help explain how it is that children in all cultures distinguish among categories of different types. Even those who suggest that children have an innate essentializing bias (e.g., Atran, 1990) acknowledge that learning must take place to determine which categories are eventually treated this way. Children have to learn the classifications of their culture, for example, that certain racial or ethnic distinctions are perceived as "deep" in their society but that other social contrasts are not.

At this point, it is important to emphasize two clarifications about these suggestions. First, positing that maternal input influences concept acquisition does *not* mean that children are passive recipients or blank slates. As noted in Chapter I, biases in maternal input can converge with children's conceptual biases (Markman, 1992). For example, as discussed earlier in this chapter, the fact that mothers differentiate domains does not mean that children fail to do so. Indeed, the implicit nature of the input suggests that mothers' and children's biases probably do converge: if children are making use of this input, they must have sufficient orienting biases to allow them to pick up on subtle cues.

The second clarification is that we do not wish to imply that parents are silent regarding the domain-specific properties that participate in information-rich theories (e.g., that members of an animal kind tend to be alike with respect to bone structure, inheritance of eye color, innate potential for height, and so forth). In fact, we believe that parents of older children probably do provide much information that may help children construct such theories. Rather, we are struck by the fact that the rich talk about categories that we have documented can be found even at a very young age when particular facts about the categories are minimal. Thus, contentful facts can be construed as details that get filled in, after children have initially established that certain categories are richly structured.

## GENERALIZABILITY ISSUES

There are a number of important issues concerning the generalizability of these results that must be considered. The first concerns the extent to which the input provided in these book-reading contexts reflects the input

these children are likely to receive in other contexts. Book reading was selected because it is apparently a richer source of information about categories
than are other contexts (Lucariello & Nelson, 1986), but book reading is also
a frequent, much practiced activity in this culture. Moreover, it is important
to note that Studies 1 and 3, which used controlled picture books that we
created, yielded results highly similar to those of Study 2, which used commercially available picture books. These similarities across studies are particularly
noteworthy given that information in the *texts* used in Study 2 showed patterns
that were very different from what mothers provided. For example, whereas
mothers provided very few similarity relations, similarity relations were common (indeed, as common as taxonomic relations) in the texts; likewise,
whereas mothers produced more taxonomic relations and generics for animals than for artifacts, the texts revealed no domain differences in this regard. Thus, patterns of maternal input are nearly constant across two dis-
tinctly different book-reading contexts despite the presence of a text that
would have encouraged different patterns.

Nonetheless, it is possible, even probable, that specifically focused contexts could elicit from mothers more talk about biological processes, internal
parts, or nonobvious similarities. Thus, the absence of these kinds of information in the book-reading session cannot be taken as evidence that they never
occur. For example, a book about the internal workings of the human body
would undoubtedly yield much talk about internal biological parts. Similarly,
a book about adoption would probably yield more discussion of origins, innate potential, and kinship relations. Although such books are presumably
rare in the libraries of young children, they become more common for older
children. Additionally, a common source of explanations and information
may be found in non-book-reading contexts. In particular, recent research
has shown that important parent-child discussions (especially, parental explanations) are initiated by children's spontaneous questions (Callanan &
Oakes, 1992). The abundance of parental explanations in such contexts contrasts with the scarcity of maternal explanations in the current studies (although differences in method make it difficult to compare frequencies directly). Therefore, it would be interesting to examine parental responses to
children's questions in light of the coding systems developed here in order
to determine the frequency of talk about biological processes, internal parts,
and nonobvious similarities.

A second issue regarding generalizability concerns the use of mothers
(not fathers) in this study. Although our initial interest was in *parental* input,
the families who participated in these studies self-selected to have mothers
rather than fathers participate. This is not surprising given that mothers were
typically the primary parents interacting with these children, as indicated by
the parental questionnaire. However, many fathers also contribute substan-

tially to their child's linguistic environment. Fathers also differ from mothers in certain aspects of their child-directed speech (Barton & Tomasello, 1994; Masur & Berko Gleason, 1980; but, for similarities, see Reese & Fivush, 1993). Thus, in the future, it would be valuable to study paternal input about categories. For example, perhaps fathers supply more factual information than mothers, or perhaps they correct children's naming errors more directly and with more explicit justification.

A third issue regarding the generalizability of these results concerns how parents from other cultural backgrounds talk to their children. Research examining language socialization has demonstrated substantial cultural variability in the kinds of speech that is directed to children (Heath, 1983; Lieven, 1994; Schieffelin & Ochs, 1986). Are the patterns obtained in the present *Monograph* universal? Are they instead specific to well-educated, middle-class U.S. samples? How do cultures differ in the sorts of input they provide? How do parents of different backgrounds discuss categories in different domains, including race, gender, and personality characteristics? Of course it is not possible to address these questions with just the present data. However, one value of this work is that it provides a framework within which comparative work can be conducted. The present studies suggest that college-educated mothers in a middle-class U.S. sample imply richly structured categories by means of generic statements, relational statements, and linking gestures. Are these devices found in other cultures? Our hope is that this work will be a starting point for investigating how and when the kinds of strategies parents use vary by language, cultural context, and content domain.

Finally, we raise the question of whether frequency in input corresponds to magnitude of effect. Specifically, does greater amount of input necessarily imply more influence on development? Although studies of language acquisition typically assume that, if input influences development, then variations in amount of input should correspond to variations in amount of language growth (e.g., Newport et al., 1977), this need not be the case. One might argue that, for certain inputs, children need to hear something from parents only once for it to have a profound influence (e.g., Carey, 1978; Heibeck & Markman, 1987; Nelson, 1987). If this is so, then the fact that parents rarely talk about origins, say, may be irrelevant to the development of this concept. What may be important is whether parents talk about origins *at all*. However, to the extent that children need hear a particular input only once to extract the relevant information (and to generalize it appropriately), it would suggest that in such cases the child is especially prepared to learn about the input in question, that it can be easily assimilated, as it were. This would once again suggest that, if children readily learn a concept on the basis of sparse and infrequent input, then they are cognitively predisposed to acquire that concept.

## CONCLUSIONS

In speech and gestures to young children (20 and 35 months of age), mothers provide much information beyond simple labeling. These sources of information are subtle yet potentially highly informative: they link different category instances (in relational statements, generics, and/or gestural links) without being explicit about how these instances are alike in important and nonobvious ways. Mothers do not seem to teach children directly that categories have essences. However, maternal input does convey that certain categories have inductive potential by focusing on certain objects not just as individuals but as members of a larger category. These data suggest possible mechanisms by which a notion of *kind* is conveyed in the absence of detailed information about category essences.

# SUPPLEMENTARY RATINGS OF PICTURE BOOKS
# USED IN STUDIES 1 AND 3

## ADULT RATINGS OF SIMILARITY

We calculated the average difference between within-category similarity and between-category similarity for each page. For example, within-category similarity is represented by the similarity between the two bats, and between-category similarity is represented by the similarity between each bat and the bird. Thus, we calculated the similarity between the two same-category instances (e.g., two bats) minus the similarity between the target-category instances and the contrasting-category instance (computed as the average of, e.g., the similarity between $bat_1$ and the bird and the similarity between $bat_2$ and the bird). Using this measure, the average difference scores are 1.08 for animals and 0.81 for artifacts ($t$ paired [11] = 2.33, $p < .05$). Note that scores could range from $-7.00$ to $+7.00$, meaning that within-category similarity and between-category similarity are fairly close for these sets.

When the average difference scores (as calculated above) are examined for each item set (i.e., page) individually, there are eight sets (four animal, four artifact) in which the average difference score is less than or equal to 0.5, six sets (three animal, three artifact) in which the average difference score is greater than 2.0, and four sets that fall in between. Thus, the animal and the artifact sets are roughly comparable, and nearly half the sets have very low scores, suggesting that the items belonging to different categories are highly similar.

We conducted a two-way ANOVA, including similarity (same category, different category) and domain (animal, artifact) as repeated-measures factors. Pairs of pictures from the same category were judged as more similar than pairs of pictures from different categories ($M$'s = 4.36 and 3.41, respectively, $F[1, 11] = 25.40$, $p < .001$). Furthermore, animals were rated as more similar overall than artifacts ($M$'s = 4.48 and 3.29, respectively, $F[1, 11] =$

61.53, $p < .0001$). Finally, there was a significant interaction between similarity and domain ($F[1, 11] = 5.43, p < .05$). The domain difference was greater for same-category pictures than for contrasting-category pictures.

## ADULT RATINGS OF THEMATIC RELATEDNESS

Animals and artifacts do not differ with respect to how close the thematic relation was between the target-category pictures and the thematic associate (calculated as an average of each target-category instance compared to the thematic associate: 5.99 for animals and 6.12 for artifacts, N.S.). Nor did animals and artifacts differ in the thematic relatedness of the contrasting-category picture and the thematic associate (2.56 for animals and 2.50 for artifacts, N.S.). Furthermore, in all 18 picture sets, the thematic relatedness of the target-category picture and the thematic associate (averaged across both target-category instances) was greater than the thematic relatedness of the contrasting-category and thematic pictures. A 2 (judgment type: target and thematic, contrasting category and thematic) $\times$ 2 (domain: animal, artifact) ANOVA revealed a main effect of judgment type ($F[1, 11] = 571.57, p < .0001$) but no effects of domain.

## CHILDREN'S MATCH-TO-SAMPLE TASK (WITHOUT LABELS)

### Participants

Thirty-two children participated (14 boys and 18 girls, ranging in age from 3–6 to 4–6; mean age 3–11), 16 per condition. An additional two children were tested but were not included, one for not completing the session, the other for not following instructions.

### Materials

Participants viewed the pages from the picture books described in Chapter II.

### Procedure

All children first received a pretest, testing their knowledge of the words *inside* and *outside*. Children were randomly assigned to one of two instructional conditions: Goes With and Insides. The wording in the Goes With task was as follows: "See this [pointing to target picture]? Which one of these [pointing to remaining three pictures] goes best with this one [pointing to target]?" For the Insides task, the wording was as follows: "See this [pointing to target]? Which one of these [pointing to remaining three pictures] has the same kinds of stuff inside as this one [pointing to target]?"

### Results

Same-category choices were selected more often than contrasting-category choices, which were selected more often than thematic choices ($M$'s = 9.28, 6.88, and 1.81, respectively, all $p$'s < .001). For each of the three choice types separately, we conducted a 2 (condition: Goes With, Insides) × 2 (domain: animals, artifacts) ANOVA. An analysis of same-category choices revealed only a main effect of domain ($F[1, 30] = 28.30$, $p < .0001$), with more same-category choices for animals than for artifacts ($M$'s = 5.37 and 3.91, respectively). Likewise, the contrasting-category analysis revealed only a main effect of domain ($F[1, 30] = 14.67$, $p < .001$), with more contrasting-category choices for artifacts than for animals ($M$'s = 3.97 and 2.91, respectively). The analysis of thematic choices revealed no effects of domain but a significant condition effect ($F[1, 30] = 7.96$, $p < .01$). There was a small but consistent tendency for participants to choose thematically more often in the Goes With condition ($M = 1.34$) than in the Insides condition ($M = 0.47$).

### Correlations with Children's Naming Data

We conducted correlations on an item-by-item basis between the children's naming data and children's choices on the present sorting task. Two correlations were conducted, one for each condition. We computed the total number of times the target- and the same-category items were given the same name (on the naming task) and the total number of times the target- and the contrasting-category items were given the same name (on the naming task), then computed a difference score. We also calculated, for each item, the number of same-category choices (on the choice task) and the number of contrasting-category choices (on the choice task), then computed a difference score. We then correlated the naming difference score with the choice difference score, on an item-by-item basis, for the Goes With and Insides conditions separately. Both correlations were high (Spearman's rho = .87 for each condition, $p < .001$). This finding suggests that children's selections of noncategory choices often reflect the belief that such choices are in fact category members.

## CHILDREN'S MATCH-TO-SAMPLE TASK (WITH LABELS)

### Participants

Twenty-five children (8 boys and 17 girls, ranging in age from 3–6 to 4–5; $M = 3$–10) participated, 13 in the Insides condition and 12 in the Goes With condition.

### Materials

The materials were identical to those of the No Label condition.

### Procedure

The tasks were identical to those of the No Label condition except that all four pictures were first labeled for the children, using the same labels as were provided for the mothers. Labels were not repeated as part of the actual question.

### Results

In contrast to the No Label study, there were more same-category choices ($M = 13.08$), fewer contrasting-category choices ($M = 4.04$), and fewer thematic choices ($M = 0.88$, all $p$'s $< .02$). However, children did not sort taxonomically across the board. When we examine children's same-category choices on an item-by-item basis, we find that the results of the No Label condition correlate highly with those of the Label condition (Spearman's rho $= .91$, $p < .01$).

For each of the three choice types separately, we conducted a 2 (condition: Goes With, Insides) $\times$ 2 (domain: animals, artifacts) ANOVA. An analysis of same-category choices revealed only a main effect of domain ($F[1, 23] = 15.98$, $p < .001$), with more same-category choices for animals than for artifacts ($M$'s $= 7.28$ and $5.79$, respectively). Similarly, the contrasting-category choices revealed only a main effect of domain ($F[1, 23] = 9.97$, $p < .005$), reflecting more contrasting-category choices for artifacts ($M = 2.57$) than for animals ($M = 1.48$). There were no significant effects for the thematic choices.

# REFERENCES

Acredolo, L., & Goodwyn, S. (1988). Symbolic gesturing in normal infants. *Child Development,* **59,** 450–466.

Adams, A. K., & Bullock, D. (1986). Apprenticeship in word use: Social convergence processes in learning categorically related nouns. In S. A. Kuczaj & M. D. Barrett (Eds.), *The development of word meaning.* New York: Springer.

Alibali, M. W., & Goldin-Meadow, S. (1993). Gesture-speech mismatch and mechanisms of learning: What the hands reveal about a child's state of mind. *Cognitive Psychology,* **25,** 468–523.

Atran, S. (1990). *Cognitive foundations of natural history: Towards an anthropology of science.* Cambridge: Cambridge University Press.

Au, T. L., Sidle, A. L., & Rollins, K. B. (1993). Developing an intuitive understanding of conservation and contamination: Invisible particles as a plausible mechanism. *Developmental Psychology,* **29,** 286–299.

Backscheider, A. B., Coley, J. C., & Gutheil, D. G. (1991, April). *The role of insides and behavior in predicting animals' appearance.* Paper presented at the meeting of the Society for Research in Child Development, Seattle.

Backscheider, A. B., Shatz, M., & Gelman, S. A. (1993). Preschoolers' ability to distinguish living kinds as a function of regrowth. *Child Development,* **64,** 1242–1257.

Balaban, M. T., & Waxman, S. R. (1997). Do word labels facilitate categorization in 9-month-old infants? *Journal of Experimental Child Psychology,* **64,** 3–26.

Baldwin, D. A., & Markman, E. M. (1989). Establishing word-object relations: A first step. *Child Development,* **60,** 381–398.

Baldwin, D. A., Markman, E. M., & Melartin, R. L. (1993). Infants' ability to draw inferences about nonobvious object properties: Evidence from exploratory play. *Child Development,* **64,** 711–728.

Barrett, S. E., Abdi, H., Murphy, G. L., & Gallagher, J. M. (1993). Theory-based correlations and their role in children's concepts. *Child Development,* **64,** 1595–1616.

Barton, M. E., & Tomasello, M. (1994). The rest of the family: The role of fathers and siblings in early language development. In C. Gallaway & B. J. Richards (Eds.), *Input and interaction in language acquisition.* Cambridge: Cambridge University Press.

Bartsch, K., & Wellman, H. M. (1995). *Children talk about the mind.* New York: Oxford University Press.

Bates, E., Benigni, L., Bretherton, I., Camaioni, L., & Volterra, V. (1979). *The emergence of symbols: Cognition and communication in infancy.* New York: Academic.

Blewitt, P. (1983). *Dog* vs. *collie:* Vocabulary in speech to young children. *Developmental Psychology,* **19,** 602–609.

Blewitt, P., & Toppino, T. C. (1991). The development of taxonomic structure in lexical memory. *Journal of Experimental Child Psychology*, **51**, 296–319.

Bloom, P. (1996). Intention, history, and artifact concepts. *Cognition*, **60**, 1–29.

Brewer, W., & Samarapungavan, A. (1991). Children's theories vs. scientific theories: Differences in reasoning or differences in knowledge? In R. Hoffman & D. Palermo (Eds.), *Cognition and the symbolic processes*. Hillsdale, NJ: Erlbaum.

Callanan, M. A. (1985). How parents label objects for young children: The role of input in the acquisition of category hierarchies. *Child Development*, **56**, 508–523.

Callanan, M. A. (1989). Development of object categories and inclusion relations: Preschoolers' hypotheses about word meanings. *Developmental Psychology*, **25**, 207–216.

Callanan, M. A. (1990). Parents' descriptions of objects: Potential data for children's inferences about category principles. *Cognitive Development*, **5**, 101–122.

Callanan, M. A. (1991). Parent-child collaboration in young children's understanding of category hierarchies. In S. A. Gelman & J. P. Byrnes (Eds.), *Perspectives on language and thought: Interrelations in development*. Cambridge: Cambridge University Press.

Callanan, M. A., & Oakes, L. M. (1992). Preschoolers' questions and parents' explanations: Causal thinking in everyday activity. *Cognitive Development*, **7**, 213–233.

Carey, S. (1978). The child as word learner. In M. Halle, J. Bresnan, & G. A. Miller (Eds.), *Linguistic theory and psychological reality*. Cambridge, MA: MIT Press.

Carey, S. (1985). *Conceptual change in childhood*. Cambridge, MA: MIT Press.

Carey, S. (1995). On the origins of causal understanding. In D. Sperber, D. Premack, & A. J. Premack (Eds.), *Causal cognition: A multidisciplinary debate*. Oxford: Clarendon.

Carlson, G. N. (1977). A unified analysis of the English bare plural. *Linguistics and Philosophy*, **1**, 413–457.

Carlson, G. N., & Pelletier, F. J. (1995). *The generic book*. Chicago: University of Chicago Press.

Clark, H. (1992). *Arenas of language use*. Chicago: University of Chicago Press.

Dahl, O. (1975). On generics. In E. L. Keenan (Ed.), *Formal semantics of natural language*. Cambridge: Cambridge University Press.

Davidson, N. S., & Gelman, S. A. (1990). Inductions from novel categories: The role of language and conceptual structure. *Cognitive Development*, **5**, 151–176.

Deák, G., & Bauer, P. J. (1995). The effects of task comprehension on preschoolers' and adults' categorization choices. *Journal of Experimental Child Psychology*, **60**, 393–427.

DeLoache, J. S., & DeMendoza, O. A. P. (1987). Joint picturebook interactions of mothers and 1-year-old children. *British Journal of Developmental Psychology*, **5**, 111–123.

Eimas, P. D., & Quinn, P. C. (1994). Studies on the formation of perceptually based basic-level categories in young infants. *Child Development*, **65**, 903–917.

Ekman, P., & Friesen, W. V. (1969). The repertoire of non-verbal behavior: Categories, origins, usage, and coding. *Semiotica*, **1**, 49–97.

Fenson, L., Dale, P. S., Reznick, J. S., Bates, E., Thal, D. J., & Pethick, S. J. (1994). Variability in early communicative development. *Monographs of the Society for Research in Child Development*, **59**(5, Serial No. 242).

Flavell, J. H., Flavell, E. R., & Green, F. L. (1983). Development of the appearance-reality distinction. *Cognitive Psychology*, **15**, 95–120.

Gelman, R. (1990). First principles organize attention to and learning about relevant data: Number and the animate-inanimate distinction as examples. *Cognitive Science*, **14**, 79–106.

Gelman, R., Durgin, F., & Kaufman, L. (1995). Distinguishing between animates and inanimates: Not by motion alone. In D. Sperber, D. Premack, & A. J. Premack (Eds.), *Causal cognition: A multidisciplinary debate*. Oxford: Clarendon.

Gelman, S. A. (1988). The development of induction within natural kind and artifact categories. *Cognitive Psychology, 20,* 65–95.

Gelman, S. A. (1996). Concepts and theories. In R. Gelman & T. K. Au (Eds.), *Handbook of perception and cognition: Vol. 13. Perceptual and cognitive development.* San Diego, Calif,: Academic.

Gelman, S. A., & Coley, J. D. (1990). The importance of knowing a dodo is a bird: Categories and inferences in 2-year-old children. *Developmental Psychology, 26,* 796–804.

Gelman, S. A., & Coley, J. D. (1991). Language and categorization: The acquisition of natural kind terms. In S. A. Gelman & J. P. Byrnes (Eds.), *Perspective on language and thought: Interrelations in development.* New York: Cambridge University Press.

Gelman, S. A., Coley, J. D., & Gottfried, G. M. (1994). Essentialist beliefs in children: The acquisition of concepts and theories. In L. A. Hirschfeld & S. A. Gelman (Eds.), *Mapping the mind: Domain specificity in cognition and culture.* New York: Cambridge University Press.

Gelman, S. A., & Gottfried, G. (1996). Causal explanations of animate and inanimate motion. *Child Development, 67,* 1970–1987.

Gelman, S. A., & Kremer, K. E. (1991). Understanding natural cause: Children's explanations of how objects and their properties originate. *Child Development, 62,* 396–414.

Gelman, S. A., & Markman, E. M. (1986). Categories and induction in young children. *Cognition, 23,* 183–209.

Gelman, S. A., & Markman, E. M. (1987). Young children's inductions from natural kinds: The role of categories and appearances. *Child Development, 58,* 1532–1541.

Gelman, S. A., & Medin, D. (1993). What's so essential about essentialism? A different perspective on the interaction of perception, language, and conceptual knowledge. *Cognitive Development, 5,* 157–168.

Gelman, S. A., & O'Reilly, A. W. (1988). Children's inductive inferences within superordinate categories: The role of language and category structure. *Child Development, 59,* 876–887.

Gelman, S. A., & Tardif, T. Z. (in press). Generic noun phrases in English and Mandarin. *Cognition.*

Gelman, S. A., & Wellman, H. M. (1991). Insides and essences: Early understandings of the non-obvious. *Cognition, 38,* 213–244.

Golinkoff, R. M., Harding, C. G., Carlson, V., & Sexton, M. E. (1984). The infant's perception of causal events: The distinction between animate and inanimate objects. In L. L. Lipsitt & C. Rovee-Collier (Eds.), *Advances in infancy research* (Vol. 3). Norwood, NJ: Ablex.

Golinkoff, R. M., Shuff-Bailey, M., Olguin, R., & Ruan, W. (1995). Young children extend novel words at the basic level: Evidence for the principle of categorical scope. *Developmental Psychology, 31,* 494–507.

Gopnik, A., & Meltzoff, A. N. (1997). *Words, thoughts, and theories.* Cambridge, MA: Bradford/ MIT Press.

Gopnik, A., & Wellman, H. M. (1994). The theory theory. In L. A. Hirschfeld & S. A. Gelman (Eds.), *Mapping the mind: Domain specificity in cognition and culture.* New York: Cambridge University Press.

Gutheil, G., & Gelman, S. A. (1997). Children's use of sample size and diversity information within basic-level categories. *Journal of Experimental Child Psychology, 64,* 159–174.

Gutheil, G., & Rosengren, K. S. (1996). A rose by any other name: Preschoolers' concept of identity across name and appearance changes. *British Journal of Developmental Psychology, 14,* 477–498.

Hayne, H., Rovee-Collier, C., & Perris, E. E. (1987). Categorization and memory retrieval by three-month-olds. *Child Development, 58,* 750–767.

Heath, S. B. (1983). *Ways with words.* Cambridge: Cambridge University Press.

Heibeck, T. H., & Markman, E. M. (1987). Word learning in children: An examination of fast mapping. *Child Development, 58,* 1021–1034.

Helweg, H. (1978). *Farm animals*. New York: Random House.

Hirschfeld, L. A. (1995a). Do children have a theory of race? *Cognition, 54,* 209–252.

Hirschfeld, L. A. (1995b). The heritability of identity: Children's understanding of the cultural biology of race. *Child Development, 66,* 1418–1437.

Hirschfeld, L. A. (1996). *Race in the making*. Cambridge, MA: MIT Press.

Hirsh-Pasek, K., & Treiman, R. (1982). Doggerel: Motherese in a new context. *Journal of Child Language, 9,* 229–237.

Horton, M. S., & Markman, E. M. (1980). Developmental differences in the acquisition of basic and superordinate categories. *Child Development, 51,* 708–719.

James, W. (1890). *The principles of psychology* (Vol. **2**). New York: Dover.

Jevons, W. S. (1877). *The principles of science* (2d ed.). New York: Macmillan.

Johnson, C. N., & Wellman, H. M. (1982). Children's developing conceptions of the mind and brain. *Child Development, 53,* 222–234.

Jones, S., & Smith, L. B. (1993). The place of perception in children's concepts. *Cognitive Development, 8,* 113–140.

Kalish, C. W. (1996a). Causes and symptoms in children's understanding of illness. *Child Development, 67,* 1647–1670.

Kalish, C. W. (1996b). Preschoolers' understanding of germs as invisible mechanisms. *Cognitive Development, 11,* 83–106.

Keil, F. C. (1986). The acquisition of natural kind and artifact terms. In W. Demopoulos & A. Marras (Eds.), *Language learning and concept acquisition*. Norwood, NJ: Ablex.

Keil, F. C. (1987). Conceptual development and category structure. In U. Neisser (Ed.), *Concepts and conceptual development: Ecological and intellectual factors in categorization*. Cambridge: Cambridge University Press.

Keil, F. C. (1989). *Concepts, kinds, and cognitive development*. Cambridge, MA: MIT Press.

Keil, F. C. (1992). The origins of an autonomous biology. In M. A. Gunnar & M. Maratsos (Eds.), *Minnesota symposium on child psychology* (Vol. **25**). Hillsdale, NJ: Erlbaum.

Keil, F. C. (1994). The birth and nurturance of concepts by domains: The origins of concepts of living things. In L. A. Hirschfeld & S. A. Gelman (Eds.), *Mapping the mind: Domain specificity in cognition and culture*. Cambridge: Cambridge University Press.

Kelemen, D. (1996). *The nature and development of the teleological stance*. Unpublished doctoral dissertation, University of Arizona.

Kohn, A. S., & Landau, B. (1990). A partial solution to the homonym problem: Parents' linguistic input to young children. *Journal of Psycholinguistic Research, 19,* 71–89.

Kripke, S. (1971). Identity and necessity. In M. K. Munitz (Ed.), *Identity and individuation*. New York: New York University Press.

Kripke, S. (1972). *Naming and necessity*. Cambridge, MA: Harvard University Press.

Kuhn, D. (1989). Children and adults as intuitive scientists. *Psychological Review, 96,* 674–689.

Lawler, J. M. (1973). Tracking the generic toad. *Papers from the ninth regional meeting of the Chicago Linguistic Society*. Chicago: Chicago Linguistic Society.

Lieven, E. V. M. (1994). Crosslinguistic and crosscultural aspects of language addressed to children. In C. Gallaway & B. J. Richards (Eds.), *Input and interaction in language acquisition*. Cambridge: Cambridge University Press.

Lin, E. L. (1996). *Thematic relations in adults' concepts and categorization*. Unpublished doctoral dissertation, University of Illinois, Champaign-Urbana.

Locke, J. (1959). *An essay concerning human understanding* (Vol. **2**). New York: Dover. (Original work published 1690)

Lopez, A., Gelman, S. A., Gutheil, G., & Smith, E. E. (1992). The development of category-based induction. *Child Development, 63,* 1070–1090.

Lucariello, J., Kyratzis, A., & Nelson, K. (1992). Taxonomic knowledge: What kind and when? *Child Development, 63,* 978–998.

Lucariello, J., & Nelson, K. (1986). Context effects on lexical specificity in maternal and child discourse. *Journal of Child Language, 13,* 507–522.

Lyons, J. (1977). *Semantics* (Vol. 1). Cambridge: Cambridge University Press.

Macnamara, J. (1986). *A border dispute.* Cambridge, MA: MIT Press.

Malt, B. C. (1994). Water is not H₂O. *Cognitive Psychology, 27,* 41–70.

Mandler, J. M. (1992). How to build a baby: 2. Conceptual primitives. *Psychological Review,* **99,** 587–604.

Mandler, J. M., & Bauer, P. J. (1988). The cradle of categorization: Is the basic level basic? *Cognitive Development, 3,* 247–264.

Mandler, J. M., Fivush, R., & Reznick, J. S. (1987). The development of contextual categories. *Cognitive Development, 2,* 339–354.

Mandler, J. M., & McDonough, L. (1996). Drinking and driving don't mix: Inductive generalization in infancy. *Cognition, 59,* 307–335.

Markman, E. M. (1989). *Categorization and naming in young children: Problems of induction.* Cambridge, MA: MIT Press.

Markman, E. M. (1991). The whole-object, taxonomic, and mutual exclusivity assumptions as initial constraints on word meanings. In S. A. Gelman & J. P. Byrnes (Eds.), *Perspectives on language and thought: Interrelations in development.* Cambridge: Cambridge University Press.

Markman, E. M. (1992). Constraints on word learning: Speculations about their nature, origins, and domain specificity. In M. R. Gunnar & M. Maratsos (Eds.), *Minnesota symposium on child psychology* (Vol. **25**). Hillsdale, NJ: Erlbaum.

Markman, E. M., & Callanan, M. A. (1984). An analysis of hierarchical classification. In R. Sternberg (Ed.), *Advances in the psychology of human intelligence* (Vol. **2**). Hillsdale, NJ: Erlbaum.

Markman, E. M., & Hutchinson, J. E. (1984). Children's sensitivity to constraints on word meaning: Taxonomic vs. thematic relations. *Cognitive Psychology, 16,* 1–27.

Marler, P. (1991). The instinct to learn. In S. Carey & R. Gelman (Eds.), *The epigenesis of mind: Essays on biology and cognition.* Hillsdale, NJ: Erlbaum.

Massey, C., & Gelman, R. (1988). Preschoolers' ability to decide whether a photographed unfamiliar object can move itself. *Developmental Psychology, 24,* 307–317.

Masur, E., & Berko Gleason, J. (1980). Parent-child interaction and the acquisition of lexical information during play. *Developmental Psychology, 16,* 404–409.

Mayr, E. (1988). *Toward a new philosophy of biology: Observations of an evolutionist.* Cambridge, MA: Harvard University Press.

McCawley, J. D. (1981). *Everything that linguists have always wanted to know about logic.* Chicago: University of Chicago Press.

McNaught, H. (1978). *The truck book.* New York: Random House.

McNeill, D. (1992). *Hand and mind.* Chicago: University of Chicago Press.

Medin, D. L. (1989). Concepts and conceptual structure. *American Psychologist, 44,* 1469–1481.

Medin, D., & Ortony, A. (1989). Comments on Part I: Psychological essentialism. In S. Vosniadou & A. Ortony (Eds.), *Similarity and analogical reasoning.* Cambridge: Cambridge University Press.

Mehler, J., & Fox, R. (Eds.). (1985). *Neonate cognition.* Hillsdale, NJ: Erlbaum.

Mervis, C. B. (1987). Child-basic object categories and early lexical development. In U. Neisser (Ed.), *Concepts and conceptual development: Ecological and intellectual factors in categorization.* Cambridge: Cambridge University Press.

Mervis, C. B., & Mervis, C. A. (1982). Leopards are kitty-cats: Object labeling by mothers for their 13-month-olds. *Child Development, 53,* 258–266.

Mervis, C. B., & Mervis, C. A. (1988). Role of adult input in young children's category evolution: 1. An observational study. *Journal of Child Language,* **15,** 257–272.

Mervis, C. B., & Rosch, E. (1981). Categorization of natural objects. *Annual Review of Psychology,* **32,** 89–115.

Mill, J. S. (1846). *A system of logic, ratiocinative and inductive.* New York: Harper & Bros.

Murphy, C. M. (1978). Pointing in the context of a shared activity. *Child Development,* **49,** 371–380.

Murphy, G. L., & Medin, D. L. (1985). The role of theories in conceptual coherence. *Psychological Review,* **92,** 289–316.

Nelson, K. (1977). The syntagmatic-paradigmatic shift revisited: A review of research and theory. *Psychological Bulletin,* **84,** 93–116.

Nelson, K. E. (1987). Some observations from the perspective of the rare event cognitive comparison theory of language acquisition. In K. E. Nelson & A. van Kleek (Eds.), *Children's language* (Vol. **6**). Hillsdale, NJ: Erlbaum.

Newport, E., Gleitman, H., & Gleitman, L. R. (1977). Mother, I'd rather do it myself: Some effects and non-effects of maternal speech style. In C. Snow & C. Ferguson (Eds.), *Talking to children: Language input and acquisition.* Cambridge: Cambridge University Press.

Ninio, A. (1980). Ostensive definition in vocabulary teaching. *Journal of Child Language,* **7,** 565–573.

Ninio, A., & Bruner, J. (1978). The achievement and antecedents of labelling. *Journal of Child Language,* **5,** 1–15.

Oakes, L. M., & Madole, K. L. (1996, April). *Making sense of infant categorization.* Paper presented at the International Conference on Infant Studies, Providence, RI.

Osherson, D. N., Smith, E. E., Wilkie, O., & Lopez, A. (1990). Category-based induction. *Psychological Review,* **97,** 185–200.

Perry, M., Church, R. B., & Goldin-Meadow, S. (1988). Transitional knowledge in the acquisition of concepts. *Cognitive Development,* **3,** 359–400.

Putnam, H. (1970). Is semantics possible? In H. E. Kiefer & M. K. Munitz (Eds.), *Language, beliefs, and metaphysics.* Albany: State University of New York Press.

Quine, W. V. (1969). Natural kinds. In W. V. Quine (Ed.), *Ontological relativity and other essays.* New York: Columbia University Press.

Quinn, P. C., Eimas, P. D., & Rosenkrantz, S. L. (1993). Evidence for representations of perceptually similar natural categories by 3-month-old and 4-month-old infants. *Perception,* **22,** 463–475.

Reese, E., & Fivush, R. (1993). Parental styles of talking about the past. *Developmental Psychology,* **29,** 596–606.

Rips, L. J. (1989). Similarity, typicality, and categorization. In S. Vosniadou & A. Ortony (Eds.), *Similarity and analogical reasoning.* Cambridge: Cambridge University Press.

Rosch, E. (1975). Cognitive representations of semantic categories. *Journal of Experimental Psychology: General,* **104,** 192–233.

Rosch, E. H., Mervis, C. B., Gray, W., Johnson, D., & Boyes-Braem, P. (1976). Basic objects in natural categories. *Cognitive Psychology,* **3,** 382–439.

Rosen, A. B., & Rozin, P. (1993). Now you see it, now you don't: The preschool child's conception of invisible particles in the context of dissolving. *Developmental Psychology,* **29,** 300–311.

Rosengren, K. S., Gelman, S. A., Kalish, C. W., & McCormick, M. (1991). As time goes by: Children's early understanding of growth in animals. *Child Development,* **62,** 1302–1320.

Rothbart, M., & Taylor, M. (1990). Category labels and social reality: Do we view social categories as natural kinds? In G. Semin & K. Fiedler (Eds.), *Language and social cognition.* London: Sage.

Schaffer, H. R., Hepburn, A., & Collis, G. M. (1983). Verbal and non-verbal aspects of mothers' directives. *Journal of Child Language*, **10**, 337–355.

Schieffelin, B. B., & Ochs, E. (Eds.). (1986). *Language socialization across cultures*. New York: Cambridge University Press.

Schnur, E., & Shatz, M. (1984). The role of maternal gesturing in conversations with one-year-olds. *Journal of Child Language*, **11**, 29–41.

Schwartz, S. P. (Ed.). (1977). *Naming, necessity, and natural kinds*. Ithaca, NY: Cornell University Press.

Schwartz, S. P. (1979). Natural kind terms. *Cognition*, **7**, 301–315.

Sera, M. D. (1992). To be or to be: Use and acquisition of the Spanish copulas. *Journal of Memory and Language*, **31**, 408–427.

Sera, M. D., Reittinger, E. L., & del Castillo Pintado, J. (1991). Developing definitions of objects and events in English and Spanish speakers. *Cognitive Development*, **6**, 119–142.

Seuss, Dr. (1960). *One fish, two fish, red fish, blue fish*. New York: Beginner Books/Random House.

Shatz, M. (1982). On mechanisms of language acquisition: Can features of the communicative environment account for development? In E. Wanner & L. Gleitman (Eds.), *Language acquisition: The state of the art*. Cambridge: Cambridge University Press.

Shipley, E. F. (1993). Categories, hierarchies, and induction. In D. Medin (Ed.), *The psychology of learning and motivation* (Vol. **30**). New York: Academic.

Siegal, M. (1988). Children's knowledge of contagion and contamination as causes of illness. *Child Development*, **59**, 1353–1359.

Siegler, R. S., & Crowley, K. (1991). The microgenetic method: A direct means for studying cognitive development. *American Psychologist*, **46**, 606–620.

Simons, D. J., & Keil, F. C. (1995). An abstract to concrete shift in the development of biological thought: The insides story. *Cognition*, **56**, 129–163.

Sloman, S. A. (1993). Feature-based induction. *Cognitive Psychology*, **25**, 231–280.

Sloman, S. A. (1994). When explanations compete: The role of explanatory coherence on judgments of likelihood. *Cognition*, **52**, 1–21.

Smiley, S. S., & Brown, A. L. (1979). Conceptual preference for thematic or taxonomic relations: A nonmonotonic age trend from preschool to old age. *Journal of Experimental Child Psychology*, **28**, 249–257.

Smith, E. E., & Medin, D. L. (1981). *Categories and concepts*. Cambridge, MA: Harvard University Press.

Smith, L. B. (1989). From global similarities to kinds of similarities: The construction of dimensions in development. In S. Vosniadou & A. Ortony (Eds.), *Similarity and analogical reasoning*. New York: Cambridge University Press.

Smith, L. B. (1992). The concept of same. In H. W. Reese (Ed.), *Advances in Child Development and Behavior*. New York: Academic.

Snow, C. E. (1972). Mothers' speech to children learning language. *Child Development*, **43**, 549–565.

Snow, C. E., & Ferguson, C. A. (Eds.). (1977). *Talking to children: Language input and acquisition*. New York: Cambridge University Press.

Snow, C. E., & Goldfield, B. A. (1983). Turn the page please: Situation-specific language acquisition. *Journal of Child Language*, **10**, 551–569.

Springer, K. (1992). Children's awareness of the biological implications of kinship. *Child Development*, **63**, 950–959.

Springer, K., & Keil, F. C. (1989). On the development of biologically specific beliefs: The case of inheritance. *Child Development*, **60**, 637–648.

Taylor, M. G. (1996). The development of children's beliefs about social and biological aspects of gender differences. *Child Development*, **67**, 1555–1571.

Tomasello, M., Anselmi, D., & Farrar, M. J. (1984/1985). Young children's coordination of gestural and linguistic reference. *First Language, 5,* 199–209.

Vosniadou, S., & Ortony, A. (1986). Testing the metaphoric competence of the young child: Paraphrase versus enactment. *Human Development, 29,* 226–230.

Wales, R., Colman, M., & Pattison, P. (1983). How a thing is called—a study of mothers' and children's naming. *Journal of Experimental Child Psychology, 36,* 1–17.

Waxman, S. R. (1990). Linguistic biases and the establishment of conceptual hierarchies: Evidence from preschool children. *Cognitive Development, 5,* 123–150.

Waxman, S. R., & Gelman, R. (1986). Preschoolers' use of superordinate relations in classification and language. *Cognitive Development, 1,* 139–156.

Waxman, S. R., & Hall, D. G. (1993). The development of a linkage between count nouns and object categories: Evidence from fifteen- to twenty-one-month-old infants. *Child Development, 64,* 1224–1241.

Waxman, S. R., & Kosowski, T. D. (1990). Nouns mark category relations: Toddlers' and preschoolers' word-learning biases. *Child Development, 61,* 1461–1473.

Waxman, S. R., & Markow, D. (1995). Words as invitations to form categories: Evidence from 12-month-old infants. *Cognitive Psychology, 29,* 257–302.

Waxman, S. R., & Namy, L. (1997). Challenging the notion of a thematic preference in young children. *Developmental Psychology, 33,* 555–567.

Waxman, S. R., Shipley, E. F., & Shepperson, B. (1991). Establishing new subcategories: The role of category labels and existing knowledge. *Child Development, 62,* 127–138.

Wellman, H. M. (1990). *The child's theory of mind.* Cambridge: Bradford/MIT Press.

Wellman, H. M., & Gelman, S. A. (1992). Cognitive development: Foundational theories of core domains. *Annual Review of Psychology, 43,* 337–375.

Wheeler, M. P. (1983). Context-related age changes in mothers' speech: Joint book reading. *Journal of Child Language, 10,* 259–263.

White, T. G. (1982). Naming practices, typicality, and underextension in child language. *Journal of Experimental Child Psychology, 33,* 324–346.

Whitehurst, G. J., Arnold, D. S., Epstein, J. N., & Angell, A. L. (1994). A picture book reading intervention in day care and home for children from low-income families. *Developmental Psychology, 30,* 679–689.

Whorf, B. L. (1945). Grammatical categories. *Language, 21,* 1–11.

Wierzbicka, A. (1994). The universality of taxonomic categorization and the indispensability of the concept "kind." *Rivista di linguistica, 6,* 347–364.

Yuill, N. (1992). Children's conceptions of personality traits. *Human Development, 35,* 265–279.

# ACKNOWLEDGMENTS

This research was supported by National Institute of Child Health and Human Development (NICHHD) grant HD-23378, National Science Foundation grant BNS-9100348, and a J. S. Guggenheim Fellowship to S. Gelman, a University of Michigan Regents Fellowship to J. Coley, and an NICHHD postdoctoral fellowship to K. Rosengren. We are very grateful to the parents and children who generously participated in the studies and to the teachers and staff of the University of Michigan Children's Centers for their able assistance. We thank Rebecca Stein, Glenn Lansky, Beth Cohen, Anne Evangelista, Cari McCarty, and Chuck Kalish for their able assistance in testing and coding, Laura Novick for supplying the picture of the boot-car, Cindy Andress for drawing Figure 1, and Moon-Ok Lee for assistance with the parent questionnaire. We also thank Marilyn Shatz, Cecelia Shore, and members of the University of Michigan Language Laboratory for comments on the work in progress, Bruce Mannheim, John Lawler, and James McCawley for references regarding generics, and Sandra Waxman and three anonymous reviewers for comments on an earlier draft. Address correspondence to Susan A. Gelman, Department of Psychology, 525 E. University Ave., University of Michigan, Ann Arbor MI 48109-1109; email: gelman@umich.edu.

# COMMENTARY

WORDS, MOMS, AND THINGS:
LANGUAGE AS A ROAD MAP TO REALITY

*Frank C. Keil*

For several years, I knew a particularly dedicated couple who routinely made the most extraordinary efforts to teach their precocious child about the world. I have vivid memories of a conversation that took place when this child was only 2 years old and had encountered a grasshopper. He said, "Jump," as the grasshopper hopped by. His parents descended on him, the mother speaking first.

"That's right, the grasshopper jumped. Well, actually he hopped; that is why he is called a 'grass*hopper*.' And do you know why he hops?"

The child looked up, but less with sparkling curiosity and more with dread of yet another pedagogical onslaught.

"He hops because he has muscles insides the legs that contract. Do you know what *contract* means?"

The child was silent, then slowly shook his head.

"*Contract* means 'to pull in.'"

"No," interrupted the father. "It means something more like shrinking quickly." He turned to the mother and discussed how contraction could be nonvolitional and how their child might be misled by her explanation.

The parents then conferred rapidly among themselves in front of the child, the mother arguing that *shrink* would further confuse, not help. After a few more interchanges and coming to an agreement on a new expositional strategy, the parents turned back to the child with zeal, who shrank back at the renewed attention.

The ensuing discussion focused on explaining how muscles worked and led to action and how they were triggered by motivation. The parents, both academics, were laboring greatly to teach the child all the unknown treasures of knowledge about grasshoppers, treasures that would explain why grasshoppers were the way they were and how hidden properties explained phenomenal ones and behaviors. The child looked ever more like a captive, eyes darting about for any alternative venue, and finally got up and ran over to a stream. The parents, noticeably exhausted from their intense efforts at explicit instruction, looked at each other in frustration, the father finally suggesting that perhaps their son was not really interested in biology and that they should try something else, like chemistry. They went over to the stream and started explaining the molecular nature of water.

### The Child's Input to the Parent

This anecdote highlights a misconception that many of us seem to have about how we can best help children learn—that we must explicitly teach them highly specific details about how the world works so that they can gradually build up out of these details more abstract thought. In this view, parents and other adults teach children by carefully explaining in a highly explicit manner the differences between categories and between instances. Perhaps, with younger children, they would speak more slowly and use simpler words and constructions; but, even with 2- and 3-year-olds, one might well expect to see parents trying to tell children what sorts of things there are, how they are to be distinguished, and why.

This *Monograph* illustrates in a masterful manner that parents do nothing of the sort or at least that mothers do not when reading picture books; and we have good reason to think that the results would extend to other situations and other groups of adults. It seems that detailed explicit instruction about the nature of the world, especially its hidden essential nature, is strikingly uncommon in adults' everyday conversations with children. Even those parents who are intensely motivated to help their children along the path of learning and who read to them for over an hour a day are still unlikely to be telling their children about all the unknown features associated with members of a category. In fact, as all but the most overzealous and academically inclined parents quickly learn, attempts to impart explicitly detailed mechanisms and principles are usually met with yawns of boredom from even the most capable of children.

The child's role in guiding the parent's language may be critical in such interactions, and even this insightful *Monograph* may not fully appreciate that influence. No one enjoys talking for long to a child who wiggles and fidgets and is increasingly disengaged from the discourse. Children tend to tell us very quickly what kind of information they need. Apparently, they do not need what armchair speculation might suggest, information about the nature of essences and hidden causes or about taxonomic relations. Instead, the mothers in these studies offered much more general guidelines that helped indicate which categories had what types of internal structures and relations to other categories and instances. Rather than provide didactic explanations of hidden properties and their consequences, parents seem to indicate in more abstract ways what sorts of things are kinds and that the kinds themselves are of different sorts.

Are the children here the real-time gatekeepers of the types and amounts of information they receive, or does the parent have a model of what to say and how to say it that arises from having observed the child over a much longer period of time? Or is such a model related less to experience with children and more to general strategies used in discourse? Several studies are suggested. Would college students with no prior experience with children show the same patterns when first asked to read to children, or would they look more like the couple described in the first paragraph of this Commentary? How would they read if they were asked to read a book to a videocamera, making a tape to be played back to a child, where there was no opportunity to receive real-time feedback? Would even experienced parents tend be more taxonomic and essentialist in the videocamera case? Answers to such questions would begin to tell us about the extent to which children actively guide the kind of linguistic information they receive.

There are strikingly few cases where a mother provides maximally explicit information, such as that an invisible property is true of all members of a category or causes phenomenal ones to be expressed. This is at first surprising given that quite young children have been found to be able to generate such statements on their own (see Wellman & Gelman, 1998). Gelman, Coley, Rosengren, Hartman, and Pappas convincingly demonstrate in this *Monograph* that, even though the children are capable of grasping details about essential properties, they do not seem to get much of that information in input and apparently do not ask for it much either. Why not? If knowing such essences seems to be the core of explanation and insight, and if the children at some level seem to appreciate that information and its special status, why do they not seek it out more aggressively, and why do parents not provide it more fully? Moreover, when parents, such as our academic couple, do provide it, why does it often seem so ineffective?

### Getting Fed Up with Explanations

Part of the answer to these questions may lie in a better characterization of what it means to have understanding and explanation in everyday life and in many of the sciences as well. We all may tend to labor under a vividness illusion. That illusion results in our thinking that we have detailed mechanistic understandings of the world around us when in fact we do not. A problem with explanation in most domains is that it is potentially unbounded in the degree to which one can provide further and further causal details responsible for an effect. The problem of explanatory regress (Harre & Madden, 1975) makes one realize that we all must confront the problem of explanatory "satiation." We cannot possibly know all the details, essentialist and otherwise, explaining all that is around us. Some more schematic representation is unavoidable (Wilson & Keil, in press). This *Monograph* starts to suggest that the ways in which children and parents talk may take into account that satiation problem. Rather than try to load the child down with what would ultimately be an impossible burden of detail, the parent is instead showing the child how to approach various domains and allowing the child to proceed to discover the details at her own pace.

Long ago, Vygotsky (1934/1986) suggested that learning concepts early on was largely a process of building information up from instances, with explicit instruction in properties and rule-like principles coming only toward the end of a concept's attainment. Only later in development did he allow for the process to be reversed, seeing older children and adults as sometimes learning concepts first through the explicit teaching of rules and principles that were later fleshed out with instances and examples. His insights are relevant to the studies in this *Monograph*. It is hardly the case that we still think of young children's concepts as merely instance-based bundles of associations; but, in our rush to embrace the idea of children as little theorists, we must realize that these theories may be far more implicit than we normally think and almost never explicitly handed to them. As Gelman et al. argue, children's rich beliefs about such things as insides, origins, and teleology are largely built up out of indirect evidence. The mothers' language may be helping greatly in more abstract ways, by indicating that things that are dissimilar on the surface might have more in common than they seem, or by suggesting that the child should look further for nonobvious relational properties; but their language does not do so more directly, perhaps just because young children's explanatory understandings are mostly not structured that way and could not be.

There is a fascinating discussion in this *Monograph* of ways in which implicit taxonomic notions might need to precede thematic ones, contrary to a very long developmental tradition claiming the opposite. Gelman et al. argue that most thematic relations presuppose taxonomic ones and that taxonomic relations are more easily inferred from perceptual and contextual clues than thematic ones. These suggestions help support an emerging reanalysis of how taxonomic and thematic relations are linked in conceptual development (e.g., Waxman & Namy, 1997). They also help us understand why an early thematic bias may sometimes appear to be present. If parents are talking about things mostly in thematic terms, children may in some tasks assume that that is the way to conduct discourse and answer experimenters' questions. Their bias sometimes to give thematic responses should no longer be equated with a conceptual bias to prefer thematic relations in understanding kinds. In addition, explicit mention of taxonomic relations to others may often appear a good deal later than implicit presupposition of those relations. Perhaps thematic relations are easier to use and mention in narrative discourse and script-like discussions (Nelson, 1988); but they may not be easier to use at a more implicit level in trying to figure out what sorts of things there are.

### Does the Information in Maternal Input Make a Difference?

This *Monograph* has such force because of the cleverness and care shown in the designs, the stimuli, and the analyses. It might seem simple enough to study how parents read to children. But, in order to illustrate the extraordinary information that might be implicitly conveyed to a child in the simple act of reading a bedtime story, one needs to specify relevant dimensions that might vary in maternal speech and that would plausibly be of value to the child. In their design and pretesting of the picture books, and in their thoughtful coding and analyses, Gelman et al. provide all of us with a superb example of how to do this kind of research. This *Monograph* will undoubtedly be a model for many other similar studies in future years.

Yet, for all its importance, it makes only more pressing the question of whether all this information in maternal speech makes a difference to children. Do children learn words and concepts differently because of the ways in which adults talk? We now see for the first time powerful new ways in which maternal speech could guide the child. It could highlight for the child which categories are likely to have richer essences. It could help the child see taxonomic relations and how they are to be contrasted with thematic ones. But does any of that information really get through to the child? Gelman et al. fully recognize that their studies do not answer this question, even as they rightly assume that there is a likely influence.

The question remains as to how one might design studies to look for a causal influence. It is a daunting problem. If the effects can occur over short time intervals, it might be possible to train parents to read picture books in two different ways and then see how those differences influence the child's understandings of kinds and categories. But this sort of study, using experimental interventions of an hour or two, might well not have any influence. Parents and others talk to children many hours a day for years. An hour or two of experimental manipulation might be a minuscule perturbation in the general pattern of learning. This has been the long-standing problem with so many training studies over the years. The length and kind of learning are often not at all ecologically valid.

Ethically and practically, one cannot ask parents to talk differently to their children for months on end. Moreover, if one were to look for different parental styles, take the most extreme contrasts, and look at the effects, many other variables would likely be causing both the language differences and the conceptual effects. But some attempts to show influences must be made because there is a real possibility that this information in parental speech is not used by the child. Perhaps, the structures that mothers use merely reflect internal cognitive place markers that help them keep track of their own speech and what they are talking about; that is, these structures are narrative mnemonic devices. In this vein, it would be useful to look more extensively at speech of this sort over a much wider range of ages. In the studies in this *Monograph*, relatively little changed in maternal speech over a period of otherwise dramatic developmental change in the children. Would that lack of change hold up for a much wider age range, assuming that appropriate books could be designed and compared across ages? If there were changes, we might have a bit more evidence of a likely causal link between reader and child.

Looking more directly at causal influence, one can envision long-term curricular contrasts in nursery schools and day-care centers, where children might receive one of two contrasting styles of language every day for 2 months during the picture-book-reading times so common in those settings. With appropriately designed picture books and carefully coached teachers, one might more plausibly ask whether these differences in language have an effect. Critical to such a design, however, would be the use of a conceptual domain that was nicely bounded and independent from domains normally discussed in the rest of the children's lives, for most of the language they would hear would still have the kinds of information found in this *Monograph* and it would be all too easy for the children to generalize inferences to categories of the same sort. Difficult as such studies will be to carry out correctly, this *Monograph* provides powerful new motivations to try to figure out a compelling design.

## Are Artifacts Cognitively Impoverished Relative to Natural Kinds?

I sit here in my living room, typing at a laptop computer and looking about. Even the plants on the mantle are artificial flowers. Nothing in view is a pure natural kind, let alone a living one. (It is dark out, so I cannot see what would otherwise be a snow-covered landscape.) Many children in developed nations spend most of their early lives in similar environments. Most things they see are human creations. They do of course see many pictorial and three-dimensional representations of natural kinds; but firsthand experience for the first several years of life may be extremely limited (except for experiencing those natural kinds known as humans). This is a radical contrast with the lives of most children a few hundred years ago and with the lives of children in some undeveloped areas today. Yet the natural world is where almost all language is more elaborated, more taxonomic, more relational, and more detailed. Graph after graph in this *Monograph* shows more complex relational information in maternal speech for living kinds than for artifacts.

Several questions arise from this experiential contrast between artifacts and living kinds and the opposing pattern of information in maternal language. Could the patterns we see in maternal language represent a compensatory mechanism targeted at children in highly developed cultures, and could children in more traditional cultures be hearing language that offers more similar patterns for artifacts and living kinds or that might even place more of an emphasis on artifacts? It seems unlikely. Parents talk about what is about them and of relevance to the child. In a culture where animals and other living and natural kinds are frequent aspects of daily life, it seems likely that speech about them would be even more frequent and elaborated relative to artifacts rather than less.

A related question concerns how patterns might differ for nonliving natural kinds. They, too, have essences in ways that artifacts do not; but the essences usually do not contribute to movement or growth. More commonly, they give rise to static phenomenal properties. The essence of gold explains its color, malleability, and density. By contrast, a tiger's essence explains not only those sorts of properties but also its shape, its patterns of movement, and many of the behaviors it engages in. In addition, the taxonomic relations among living kinds are vastly more powerful and inductively important than those among nonliving natural kinds (Atran, 1996). (The periodic table is hardly a neat taxonomic hierarchy.) If the picture books in these studies had included nonliving natural kinds, like a gem or a star, how might they be discussed relative to living kinds and artifacts? My guess is that the natural kind status is especially important and that the language would point out their special status as natural kinds but also as different from living ones; but that remains only a tentative guess. We have reason to believe that young children do appreciate the special status of nonliving natural kinds in contrast to both living kinds and artifacts (Keil, Smith, Simons, & Levin, 1998). Do the parents also honor those differences in the ways in which they use their language?

Why do mothers engage in such speech and provide richer information about living kinds? The answer is not obvious. It is not, for example, evident that the world of animals and all that they relate to is so much more cognitively complex than the world of artifacts. To be sure, most natural kinds may have richer internal structures than most artifacts, but most artifacts may have richer sociocultural contexts in which they are causally related. Thus, artifacts and their properties may be less related causally to "inner" properties but more related to intentions, needs, goals, desires, and aptitudes of human agents and to the properties of the society and culture at large.

Why should one relational cluster evoke less elaborated and informative talk than another? One possibility is that the essentialist bias includes not only an assumption that things have essences but also an assumption that such essences are related to the most important things to talk about, namely, stable phenomenal properties of things. One talks about not the essences directly but rather all the things that are causally connected to them, usually as consequences. This sort of bias seems similar to the "fundamental attribution error" in that it may reflect a bias to focus on dispositional properties and their consequences rather than on more situational ones, which are so central to artifacts (cf. Peng & Nisbett, in press). Given claims of large cross-cultural differences in such a bias (Miller, 1996), the possibility remains that adults in other cultures might talk in more complex ways about artifacts for reasons having to do with different default biases in relative emphases on situational and dispositional factors. As said earlier, I doubt that such differences will be pronounced; but, clearly, the need for cross-cultural work is compelling.

### The Benefits of Being Vague and Abstract—on Perceiving Patterns Rather than Being Told Them

This *Monograph* reveals a fascinating and surprisingly understated and subtle way of imparting information about category types and their natures. Quite abstract properties and relations are often conveyed in the patterns of discourse while rarely being explicitly laid out. It almost seems as if the parents are teasing the children as they dance around all the meaty details, sometimes perversely providing more thematic descriptions of the objects around them than the children do themselves. In this Commentary, I have tried to suggest that this parental behavior is not perverse and that parental speech may be of just the right sort to help children learn optimally. Children need to control their own pace of acquisition of mechanistic details and principles. Neither they nor we can master all the details, so they must be highly judicious in deciding when to look deeper and learn more. We do not yet know whether they have helped shape up parents by disengaging when such details start to flood them or whether the parents for other reasons avoid offering such floods of explicit information. It does seem clear that it is far too difficult for parents to know at any time what a child's needs might be with respect to detailed information; so, in the absence of a highly specific request for information, it would be far preferable to try to provide a kind of rough road map to reality and to do so at a level of abstraction that allows it to be useful for a very wide range of situations and instances that the child might later encounter on her own.

These road maps may tell the child what kind of cognitive stance to adopt for a class of things. Gelman et al. have also set up their own road map for those of us concerned with conceptual development. Their studies now allow us to see a host of new ways in which a child might be helped in making sense of the world through patterns implicitly conveyed in discourse. Just as the child must actively follow up on the parents' implicit cues, it remains for us in the field to follow up on the many research suggestions implicit in this work.

## References

Atran, S. (1996). From folk biology to scientific biology. In D. R. Olson & N. Torrance (Eds.), *Handbook of education and human development: New models of learning, teaching, and schooling.* Cambridge, MA: Blackwell.

Harre, R., & Madden, E. H. (1975). *Causal powers: A theory of natural necessity.* Totowa, NJ: Rowman & Littlefield.

Keil, F., Smith, C., Simons, D., & Levin, D. (1998). Two dogmas of conceptual empiricism. *Cognition, 65,* 103–135.

Miller, J. G. (1996). Culture as a source of order in social motivation: Comment. *Psychological Inquiry, 7,* 240–243.

Nelson, K. (1988). The ontogeny of memory for real events. In U. N. E. Winograd (Ed.), *Remembering reconsidered: Traditional and ecological approaches to the study of memory.* New York: Cambridge University Press.

Peng, K., & Nisbett, R. E. (in press). Cross-cultural similarity and difference in understanding physical causality. In M. Shale (Ed.), *Culture and Science.* Lanham, MA: University Press of America.

Vygotsky, L. S. (1986). *Thought and language.* Cambridge, MA: MIT Press. (Original work published 1934)

Waxman, S. R., & Namy, L. (1997). Challenging the notion of thematic bias in young children. *Developmental Psychology, 33,* 555–567.

Wellman, H. M., & Gelman, S. (1998). Knowledge acquisition in foundational domains. In D. Kuhn & R. Siegler (Eds.), *Handbook of child psychology: Vol. 2. Cognition, perception and language* (5th ed.). New York: Wiley.

Wilson, R. A., & Keil, F. C. (in press). The shadows and shallows of explanation. *Minds and Machines.*

# CONTRIBUTORS

**Susan A. Gelman** (Ph.D. 1984, Stanford University) is professor of psychology at the University of Michigan, Ann Arbor. She is on the editorial boards of *Cognitive Psychology,* the *Developmental Review,* the *Merrill-Palmer Quarterly,* and the *Michigan Quarterly Review.* Her research interests include early cognitive development and relations between language and thought.

**John D. Coley** (Ph.D. 1993, University of Michigan) is a postdoctoral fellow at Northwestern University. His research interests include cognitive development, cultural differences in categorization and reasoning, and effects of expertise on cognition.

**Karl S. Rosengren** (Ph.D. 1989, University of Minnesota) is assistant professor of psychology and kinesiology at the University of Illinois, Champaign-Urbana. His research interests include cognitive and motor development.

**Erin Hartman** (M.S. 1994, Boston University) is the managing editor of the Clinical Crossroads series of the *Journal of the American Medical Association.*

**Athina Pappas** (M.D. 1998, Wayne State University) is currently a medical resident at Children's Hospital of Michigan.

**Frank C. Keil** (Ph.D. 1977, University of Pennsylvania) is the W. R. Kenan Jr. Professor of Psychology at Cornell University. Much of his recent work focuses on the roles of explanation and causal understanding in structuring concepts and guiding their acquisition. He is the author of *Semantic and Conceptual Development: An Ontological Perspective* (1979) and *Concepts, Kinds and Cognitive Development* (1989).

# STATEMENT OF EDITORIAL POLICY

The *Monographs* series is intended as an outlet for major reports of developmental research that generate authoritative new findings and use these to foster a fresh and/or better-integrated perspective on some conceptually significant issue or controversy. Submissions from programmatic research projects are particularly welcome; these may consist of individually or group-authored reports of findings from some single large-scale investigation or of a sequence of experiments centering on some particular question. Multiauthored sets of independent studies that center on the same underlying question can also be appropriate; a critical requirement in such instances is that the various authors address common issues and that the contribution arising from the set as a whole be both unique and substantial. In essence, irrespective of how it may be framed, any work that contributes significant data and/or extends developmental thinking will be taken under editorial consideration.

Submissions should contain a minimum of 80 manuscript pages (including tables and references); the upper limit of 150–175 pages is much more flexible (please submit four copies; a copy of every submission and associated correspondence is deposited eventually in the archives of the SRCD). Neither membership in the Society for Research in Child Development nor affiliation with the academic discipline of psychology are relevant; the significance of the work in extending developmental theory and in contributing new empirical information is by far the most crucial consideration. Because the aim of the series is not only to advance knowledge on specialized topics but also to enhance cross-fertilization among disciplines or subfields, it is important that the links between the specific issues under study and larger questions relating to developmental processes emerge as clearly to the general reader as to specialists on the given topic.

Potential authors who may be unsure whether the manuscript they are planning would make an appropriate submission are invited to draft an outline of what they propose and send it to the Editor for assessment. This mechanism, as well as a more detailed description of all editorial policies, evaluation processes, and format requirements, is given in the "Guidelines for the Preparation of *Monographs* Submissions," which can be obtained by writing to the Editor, Rachel K. Clifton, Department of Psychology, University of Massachusetts, Amherst MA 01003.

| DATE DUE | |
|---|---|
| MAR 23 2009 | |
| | |
| | |
| | |
| | |
| | |
| | |
| | |
| | |
| | |
| | |
| | |
| | |
| | |
| | |
| | |
| | |
| | |

GAYLORD                                    PRINTED IN U.S.A.